PLAIN WRAPPED
ANOINTING

Unleashing the Miraculous in a Different Way

GEORGE PANTAGES

in person

Healing hand

George Pantages Ministries

George Pantages Ministries

George Pantages
Cell 512 785-6324
geopanjr@yahoo.com
Georgepantages.com

TABLE OF CONTENTS

consecrating to high office

DEDICATION

I would like to dedicate this book to my daughters Stephanie and Christi:

Stephanie (Fluffy) - You have always had the ability to make me laugh even to this day after all of the "ugly" we have had to put up with. I believe that your crazy ways and how you express yourself have been the crutch I have needed to lean on when I really just wanted to end it all. They say that laughter is the best medicine and who can deny that because when we are together laughing, everything in the world is fine. My one word of advice to you would be to use this God given gift for His Glory so the rest of the world can laugh along as well.

Christi (One-o) - You move me in ways that make me desire to draw closer to God. Your loving, gentle, kindness truly is Christ-like. I know you don't see it because it's easier to dwell on your shortcomings, but someday you will. When that day finally comes you'll understand why Daddy named you Christi with an "I". Keep your eyes open because that day is not too far away.

I love you both ever so much and would just like to say that I wouldn't trade either of you for the world!

SPONSORS

I would like to take the time to appreciate the following people for their contribution on the publication of this book:

Antonio Bojorquez
Pastor Luis Perez
Joe Rivera
Pastor Rodolfo Guia
Pastor Benjamin & Silvia Guerra
Pastor Porfirio Mayorquin
Richard & Terry Cantu
Gustavo & Tangie Villagrana
Louis J. Robles
Della Steel
Justina Rubio

Michelle Levigne – Editor

INTRODUCTION

Plain is not the way that any of us would like to be perceived. Whether we are talking about our looks, the way we dress, how we talk, or where we live etc. etc. etc. Plain is just not acceptable. Why, because no one wants to lack beauty, or to be considered ordinary in any way especially if that means reaching the level of ugly. The definition of "plain" is pretty much relative, taking into consideration the eye of the beholder. What might be perfect in one's eye is ghastly in another's. It is then imperative we find out what God wants and adjust ourselves accordingly.

It is this assault on what God sees as acceptable that keeps Satan completely focused without ever giving up. If the distractions of life can bump us just enough from the perfect will of God then he will have accomplished his goal. He needn't lead us into gross sin but to pervert our thinking which will eventually lead us away from the pureness of the Gospel.

I marvel that you are turning away so soon from Him who called you in the grace of Christ, to a different gospel, which is not another; but there are some who trouble you and want to pervert the gospel of Christ. (Gal 1:6-7)

Timing with God is everything. For that same reason Satan works overtime, triggering delays of all sorts. Whether they are uncontrollable circumstances, extending a waiting period, or just Satan being Satan, they are all part of his bag of tricks. Moments of indecision can knock the timing of God's will out of whack and allow a counterfeit anointing rule where it has no jurisdiction.

Counterfeit anointing has become the craze of this generation because it is so easy to be had. With a good education and a bag full of talent, who needs a plain wrapped anointing? If we are ever going to see our God produce the signs and wonders that the first century Church experienced, our focus must return to its roots. We must lift up the name of Jesus the way our forefathers did. In its simplicity it is powerful enough to bring this entire world to its knees. Plain and simple, that's how God works the best!

CHAPTER 1

Where Are God's Anointed?

*So I sought for a man among them who would make
a wall, and stand in the gap before Me on behalf of
the land, that I should not destroy it; but I found no
one.*   *(Ezek 22:30)*

On the sixth week of our trip through three states, we
pulled our rental car into the driveway of a pastor's home
where we would be staying for the next couple of days. As
we went about our business, coming and going to different
churches every day, something out of the ordinary
happened on the third day. Unbeknownst to us, the pastor's
neighbor had been eyeing us all this time, watching our
every move. Thursday night's service was in a church only
a few blocks away, lo and behold, she was in church that
night with her children. When it came time to pray for the
sick, she got into the line. She did not heal during the first
phase of ministry, so we proceeded to the next phase.
(Note: In my ministry, if after two prayers those who are
feeling pain do not heal, I conclude that their pains are not
physical and consequently begin to deal with emotional and
spiritual problems. At this level, ministry becomes more
personal and I deal with each person secretly in their ear, to
avoid any kind of embarrassment.)

Why She Would Not Heal

In actuality, the back pain that she was suffering from initially was healed, but there was something else that God wanted to deal with. Of course she was still suffering from a great amount of pain in her jaw, and with a word of knowledge, I understood why. She was verbally abusing a man who had broken her heart years ago and her spewing of venom was relentless. God had determined not to heal her until the verbal assassinations ceased. As I whispered all of this into her ear, her face began to redden and the tears slowly began to stream down her cheeks. She could not hide this from God no matter what she said or did, neither could she escape His wrath. The pain in her jaw was the result of her loose tongue and her torment was in actuality God-sent.

Then his master, after he had called him, said to him, 'You wicked servant! I forgave you all that debt because you begged me. Should you not also have had compassion on your fellow servant, just as I had pity on you?' And his master was angry, and delivered him to the torturers until he should pay all that was due to him. "So My heavenly Father also will do to you if each of you, from his heart, does not forgive his brother his trespasses."

(Matt 18:32-35)

She humbled herself, admitting her wrong, and in doing so the Lord immediately healed her. Her faith grew to such proportions that when it came time to pray for those who were seeking the Holy Ghost, she too came to the altar and was baptized in the Spirit, speaking in other tongues.

A Surprising Confession

As the altar call was winding down, my wife made her way to the back of the church as she normally does, to sell

10

our books. It was at this time that we heard the rest of the story. That same woman, somewhat embarrassed, confessed to my wife that she had been observing us for the last three days. From the time of our arrival stepping out of our car, she could sense that there was something different about us, causing her heart to yearn more for God. She then made a decision to visit for the first time the church that was just a few blocks away. When she walked into the sanctuary that Thursday night, she could not believe God had sent her to the same church that I was going to be ministering at. It was then that she knew the Lord had something special for her that evening. It was our anointing that drew her near and gave her the opportunity to experience Christ in a way that she had never ever thought possible.

Anointing! It is the one thing in the kingdom of God that makes all the difference in the world. Much like wisdom, it must be obtained at all costs. It keenly sharpens our talents and gifts. It heightens our sensitivity to the voice of God and His Spirit, being aware of circumstances and situations that would under normal conditions fly right past us. But what is anointing? How is it acquired? Is it available to any and all children of God? Let us take a journey back into the Old Testament to find its origin, its physical and spiritual implications, and hopefully a present-day application of this much-needed gift that is scarcely found in the world today.

Preparing Oil in the Old Testament

The anointing oil used in the Old Testament was specially prepared for a special event. The sanctuary oil applied for this purpose was not the run of the mill oil, consumed for daily use. It featured green, unripe olives that were extracted from trees in mountainous areas[1]. They were extremely difficult to find, and the whole process

11

from beginning to end was slow, painstaking, and particularly arduous, to say the least.

The conversion of the olive to this special oil was not complete until the olive itself was entirely crushed or trodden. Taking into consideration all that was needed to manufacture this precious oil, it was truly considered a gift from God. On the other hand, symbolically, it was a constant reminder that the call of God came to the unassuming, inexperienced man as well, provided that he was willing to be absolutely crushed, allowing God's anointing to break the yoke. With the process concluded, this distinctive oil could only be applied upon prophets, priests, or kings.

When the Oil Was Applied

The actual anointing was an event to be witnessed by many, usually in a public place. It must be duly noted that the practice of anointing has changed considerably from Old Testament times. Whereas today a dab of oil is sufficient to complete the ceremony, it was not so in this biblical period. An entire flask of oil (*keren*, 1-2 gallons) [2] was used to pour over the head of the recipient. The oil would find its way down his face, onto his beard, saturating his clothing with an unmistakable fragrance that would linger. There would never be a doubt in anyone's mind that this man had been anointed. From that day forward, there was a mark upon him that would separate him unto God from the rest of humanity. It was a mark he could not deny nor hide.

The most significant message that God could convey to us is that in anointing one of His servants, the anointing itself would always include brokenness.

A Common Problem Today

That being said, it brings us to the greatest problem we face today. There is way too much ministering amongst us without a genuine anointing. Who in their right mind would attempt such a crime? I say "a crime" because an anointing upon a child of God has always symbolized the unrestricted flowing of the Spirit of God through us[3]. There cannot be a mightier power promised that can provide the victory we seek when satanic opposition rears its ugly head. Yet, we seem to follow the lead of our biblical ancestors, failing miserably in solving the problems that leave us dazed. They too lacked a genuine anointing; they never allowed the Lord to bring them into a place of complete brokenness.

The children of Israel did not know how to handle the period of waiting that was pressed upon them when Moses went up to Mount Sinai. Their restlessness turned into grumbles, which in turn began to spell trouble for Aaron, the priest left in charge while Moses was away. Their complaints put him in a quandary, because although they were yearning to worship God, they were asking him to produce a god they could actually see. To soothe their anxiety, he built them a golden calf and what happened next was frightening.

> Then *they* said, "This is *your* god, O Israel that brought you out of the land of Egypt!" So when Aaron saw it, he built an altar before it. And Aaron made a proclamation and said, "Tomorrow is a feast to the LORD." Then they rose early on the next day, offered burnt offerings, and brought peace offerings; and the people sat down to eat and drink, and rose up to play (Ex 32:4-6)

Aaron's *Grave* Mistake

It's bad enough that Aaron succumbed to the cries of this backslidden bunch and built them a god they could see. But the next sequence of events surely proves that ministering without anointing leads to disaster. You would have thought that when the children of Israel had

13

proclaimed their new god as the God that had brought them out of Egypt, it would have immediately raised red flags in the mind of Aaron. Because the Spirit of God was not leading him to do what was right, he could not discern the difference, and he continued going through his normal routine of making sacrifices. He had completely lost track of the meaning of this sacred task, allowing it to become nothing more than a mere ritual. When God had established burnt offerings as a sacrifice unto Him, it was implied that there would be a complete surrender in unreserved devotion unto Him, Jehovah. Peace offerings, on the other hand, were created to bring both parties to a reconciling place of peace[4]. Obedience to the commandments of God must be done in the right spirit or they become nothing more than going through the motions, which in turn are unacceptable to the Master.

When those of us today who are called to ministry begin to minister without an anointing, our ability to discern truth is weakened. The revelation of knowing the one true God is lost, all gods and religions become common, and we come to the conclusion that there is no bona fide difference. We are blinded to believe that as long as there is sincere worship, nothing else really matters.

Can you understand now why God is looking for anointed men and women in the times that we live? There is an all out war going on, one that takes no prisoners. If it is to be won handily, it must be fought on God's terms, using the best that Heaven has to offer.

For the weapons of our warfare are not carnal but mighty in God for pulling down strongholds, casting down arguments and every high thing that exalts itself against the knowledge of God...

(2 Cor 10:4,5)

For all that we war against, there is no match for an anointed child of God. Armed, dangerous, and fully equipped are the unrivaled credentials the enemy must deal with, battling with God's chosen people. The anointing will break any and all barriers that try to impede the blessings of God's promises to His children. *....and the yoke shall be destroyed because of the anointing.* (Isa 10:27 KJV) That, my friend, is not a threat, it is a promise.

An Even Greater Mistake

As distressing as it is to ponder the notion that spiritual battles are being fought daily without an anointing, it is an even greater tragedy to realize that there are children of God with a great anointing not ever knowing that it is available to them. This is the exact situation that Gideon found himself in when the call of God took place. Look at Gideon's words when, as a complete shock and in total disagreement, he rejected God's appeal.

And the Angel of the LORD appeared to him, and said to him, "The LORD is with you, you mighty man of valor!" ...Then the LORD turned to him and said, "Go in this might of yours, and you shall save Israel from the hand of the Midianites. Have I not sent you?" So he said to Him, "O my Lord, how can I save Israel? Indeed my clan is the weakest in Manasseh, and I am the least in my father's house.
(Judg 6:12,14-15)

It wasn't enough for an angel of the Lord to appear to him personally with a candid declaration from God Himself. With that message being rejected, the Lord took the bull by the horns and spoke directly to this man of God, who did not have a clue as to what God had deposited in his soul. As forthright as God could be, Gideon still had his doubts and was coy with God.

15

> *...God, who gives life to the dead and calls those things which do not exist as though they did;*
>
> (Rom 4:17)

Gideon was hopelessly oblivious to the plans and purpose that God had designed specifically for his life. If only Gideon could have seen how God saw him, he would not have been so apprehensive to accept the outlines for greatness that would define his life for an eternity. But even the greatest of anointing cannot be released without faith. God was willing to put up with these deficiencies of faith, knowing that with the baby steps Gideon was willing to take, it would eventually catapult him to the spiritual dominance God had in mind from the beginning.

Gideon's Schooling Begins

The lessons began when God raised fire from the rock and consumed Gideon's sacrifice. The Lord, with a great show of patience, put dew on some fleece, then reversed the process on the following day. It was immediately after this show of power that an anointing fell upon Gideon, unleashing a newfound faith. The armies of Israel recognized a bold confidence in their leader that was not there in the past, and were willing to follow him into battle without any reservation whatsoever.

Faith-driven anointing will take you to places where most people will not be allowed to go. This type of anointing will leapfrog you into levels of preeminence that most people only dream about. It will help you to accomplish feats that in the eyes of others are classified and hidden in the archives of the impossible. That is why I believe when Gideon asked 22,000 troops to go home, leaving him with a mere 10,000 men to fight, those who remained didn't bat an eyelash. When this courageous warrior continued to whittle down his army to a paltry 300, it did not rattle the survivors. Why, you might ask? One did not have to count heads to understand that the battle was in their favor once an anointing had fallen upon them. *What then shall we say to these things? If God is for us, who can be against us?* (Rom 8:31) With God and His anointing flowing freely, the devil doesn't stand a chance.

A Breaking Takes Place

It was written earlier in the chapter that breaking and/or brokenness is essential to giving free rein to God's anointing in our lives. Gideon's victory over the Midianites confirms that fact. It was when he accepted the challenge to lead Israel into battle that his will was broken. In order for him to accomplish what God had sent him to do, one more breaking needed to take place. He separated his 300 men, arming them with nothing more than a trumpet and an earthen vessel with a torch inside. At the designated signal, the 300 men followed Gideon's lead, blowing their trumpets and breaking their vessels. Who in their right mind would have believed this stunt had any chance to succeed? An anointed child of God would have, and without lifting a finger, Gideon and his men watched in amazement as the Spirit of the Lord brought a great confusion upon the Midianite camp, causing them to kill each other.

It is astounding to think how much God could accomplish on this earth if only He could find more people willing to be broken and anointed. He already has what is needed to make this work, you and I. He shouldn't have to be forced into putting a gun to our heads when the efforts He made to reveal Himself to us at the time of salvation should have been sufficient. When He sought us out, it was more than a casual look. He knew who He wanted, where to find us, and how to get our attention. We were handpicked and carefully chosen.

You did not choose Me, but I chose you and appointed you that you should go and bear fruit, and that your fruit should remain, that whatever you ask the Father in My name He may give you.

(John 15:16)

The stage has been set to unleash God's glory, one anointed person at a time. What is holding back the floodgates of heaven, restricting this overflow of anointing? I believe it is our feelings of inadequacy that short-circuit that flow. We react very much the same as the character in a story I heard years ago.

A particular earthen vessel was finally bought from the potter who had kept it on display in the front window. Sadly to say, the new owner brought it back after a couple of days, complaining that the oil inside tasted very much like the vessel itself. The taste was so strong that it was taking away the sweetness of the oil. The potter, in total embarrassment, rushed to make the exchange, putting the vessel back on the shelf. Feeling somewhat worthless, the vessel came to the conclusion that it would never be good enough. But something began to happen the longer it sat on the shelf. The oil began to penetrate the walls of the vessel, sealing off the ingredients that were diluting the taste of the oil. In other words, a breaking was taking place, changing the entire makeup of a vessel that appeared insignificant. Without the breaking, the vessel would have never reached its potential. With it, it became the valuable commodity the potter had in mind when he created it in the beginning.

Identifying with Brokenness

I can pretty much identify with this vessel, because my entire life has been filled with a lot of brokenness. At the age of 5 when polio struck my body, this deadly disease left its crippling marks. My right arm was left withered and my right leg slightly longer than my left. My upper body

18

lacked strength, so as I grew older, the shape of my body morphed into that of a pear-like silhouette. The emotional scars left by this illness are ones that have yet to be conquered. You can say that as a child, my body was broken.

There are several occurrences in my life that have caused my spirit to be broken. I could probably write an entire book on this one subject. Time and time again throughout my life, I have been put back on the potter's wheel in order to be reformed and reshaped. The purpose for this breaking has always been for the same reason, reshaping me to look more like my Savior. I remember several times after being broken so harshly that I said to myself, I don't think that I could go through anything else that would hurt me as much as this has. Then unexpectedly, something came out of the blue to cause an even deeper pain that only the grace of God could heal.

I could never imagine hurting with so much anguish when my first marriage ended in divorce. The pain that I was asked to tolerate was not only intense and bewildering, it also persisted for what appeared like an eternity. The hopelessness and despair lead to great depressions. I chronicled in my first book, *An Evil Day,* the thoughts of suicide that began to run rampant in my head every day. They increased in number until the breaking was complete. You could say when the five years of separation from my first wife ended in divorce, my spirit was completely broken.

It was at this point that the Lord moved to complete the trifecta, breaking one's will. This is the stage where we take on the attitude the Lord Himself displayed in the garden of Gethsemane. He exhibited an unwillingness to die by the prayer He prayed three times to the Father.

3 times *Three times prayed*

"O My Father, if it is possible, let this cup pass from Me; nevertheless, not as I will, but as You will." (Matt 26:39)

When His will was finally broken, the strength to endure the brutal death at Calvary was embraced and He completed the mission He was brought into this world for.

Humbling yourself so that your will might be broken is arguably the most difficult of all forms of breaking. For whatever it's worth, we have an agenda that is pretty much set in stone, and even letting God adjust it is not an option. It is for this very reason that God will break our spirit first to prepare us for the most important breaking we will ever experience.

When the dust settled and my evil day was behind me, I had considered the notion with my new life that I could possibly return to pastoring, which was my first love. There were many of my new wife's family who had still not accepted the Lord, and on the surface it appeared like a great place to start. Lo and behold, the Lord had other plans. Not only were we not going to pastor, we were asked to move away from family to the state of Texas where we knew no one. If it were not for the fact that I had just come out of a breaking so grueling and taxing, I would have put up so much more of a fight. As it turned out, I humbled myself without a whimper. The final breaking of my will unwrapped the purest, most powerful anointing I have ever experienced. Without a shadow of a doubt, when we made our move to Texas, my will was broken.

So I sought for a man among them who would make a wall, and stand in the gap before Me on behalf of the land, that I should not destroy it; but I found no one. (Ezek 22:30)

Finding a Man

The reason why the Lord had such a difficult time finding someone to make up that wall was because a wall must be made out of hewn stone. Hewn stones were given form or shape with heavy cutting blows. Now I know that the Lord was talking figuratively, nevertheless, no one wants to enter into ministry if it will take severe blows to conform to His image. We hate to admit it, but that's just His way of doing business. If you're going to be anointed and mightily used of God, you must be willing to be broken.

Isn't it time you allowed the Lord to break you so that He can anoint you? Take the words of John the Baptist to heart when he said, *He must increase, but I must decrease.* (John 3:30) You needn't worry that at this point people will see more of you than the Christ who lives inside. You'll get to the place where the anointing will overflow, and all they'll see is Jesus.

End Notes

[1.] Manners and Customs of the Bible, Beaten Oil
[2.] Bodner, 1 Samuel, Pg 93
[3.] 1John 2:20, 27
[4.] Nelson's Bible Dictionary, Sacrificial Offerings

CHAPTER 2

We're Only Halfway There
(FOR MINISTERS ONLY)

in mighty signs and wonders, by the power of the Spirit of God, ... I have fully preached the gospel of Christ. (Rom 15:19)

P aying the full price for anything seems so un-American. If we have not been schooled in the art of negotiation, our upbringing has been sorely limited. Why? Because everything in life is negotiable. I had my first lessons in this art as a young boy, curiously watching my father navigate his way to lower prices when we visited the border town of Tijuana. It wasn't so much that we could not afford paying the asking price, but rather the principle of knowing that you could purchase something for far less than what it was worth. I learned at an early age that if at all possible, never pay full price.

It appears that Jacob came from the same school of thought. Conniving, dickering, and haggling were all a part of his gamut in negotiating his way to a better life. His pieces of good fortune would go vastly under-appreciated if they had not been secured by some kind of deviant struggle. If there was ever a man who lived up to his name, truly it was he. Yet it is utterly mind-boggling to reflect on

23

the fact that there are many in ministry today belonging to the same fraternity. The call of God in a person's life cannot be negotiated; it must be done on His terms

No Negotiating Here.

Elijah deliberately complained to the Lord after the Mount Carmel massacre, banking on the fact that his protests were legitimate enough to bring pity upon this prophet in distress. Listen to their conversation:

And he said, "I have been very zealous for the LORD God of hosts; because the children of Israel have forsaken Your covenant, torn down Your altars, and killed Your prophets with the sword. I alone am left; and they seek to take my life."

The Lord in turn responds with this: *Yet I have reserved seven thousand in Israel, all whose knees have not bowed to Baal, and every mouth that has not kissed him.* (1 Kings 19:14,18) In other words, the Lord was bluntly stating the fact that if this yellow-bellied prophet did not like the conditions or the terms of this position, he could easily be replaced. His replacement would be hungrier, more passionate, and above all willing to comply with all that the Lord was asking of him. He just needed to say the word and the appropriate arrangements could be made.

Understanding that negotiating with God is not an option, we must also bear in mind that the call to ministry must be complete. It is imperative we grasp the realization that our ministries should incorporate the mighty signs and wonders the early Church utilized in everyday life. Thayer's Greek Lexicon defines the phrase ("fully preach" in Romans 15:19 to simply mean, "to cause God's will to be obeyed as it should be, to make complete." If that be true, and it is put to the test in our ministries, we must woefully admit that we are only halfway there.

Moving in the Wrong Direction

In continuing our scrutiny of our ministries today, it is ever so critical to be ministering in the power of the Holy Ghost. As I speak to those, like myself, with a Pentecostal heritage we must come to grips with the fact that the understanding of this concept has been somewhat skewed by our undaunted pursuit of the moving of that same Spirit. Ministering in the power of the Spirit includes a lot more than a Holy Ghost two-step on a Sunday night. A powerful move of God's Spirit should lead us to the unleashing of His gifts, which in turn allows the miraculous through the anointing to save, heal, and fill with the Holy Ghost. Miracles, signs, and wonders should be the norm, not the exception.

What I am advocating is not necessarily a new belief. I'm sure it can be traced throughout church history. Nevertheless, because we have not experienced this in our own lifetime, it falls by the wayside, never to be used and taken advantage of. We more willingly accept time-tested myths, keeping us in comfort zones that cannot be easily penetrated by newfangled ideas. One of these myths is that ministries begin and end with preaching. Focus on good preaching is greater than ever before. Of course, the benefit of raising good young preachers goes without saying. The mantra for this generation could surely be, *Study to shew thyself approved unto God, a workman that needeth not to be ashamed, rightly dividing the word of truth.* (2 Tim 2:15 KJV) There is a common goal that has begun to materialize right before our eyes in that these new crops of preachers believe they will be better than their mentors, that indeed is their driving force. The downside to this is that a faction is being raised where the specialization of preaching has negated any efforts to minister. They are silver-tongued in their oratory, yet deficient in the power of the Spirit. As I have mentioned before, we are settling for a move of the

25

Holy Ghost when He would like to go one step further to unleash His glory.

Paul Couldn't Get His Point Across Either

The Apostle Paul encountered similar problems with the Corinthians. They were being puffed up by their own "words". Although the apostle went out of his way to set an example that could be easily followed once he left, they had made a decision to go in another direction. There was a reason the apostle was so adamant in his instructions, *Therefore I urge you, imitate me.* (1 Cor 4:16)

His ministry was predicated on power, not words. Paul's comprehension of spiritual things was exceedingly beyond that of his Corinthian disciples, shown by his words to them in chapter 4 verse 20: *For the kingdom of God is not in word but in power.* These words would also be somewhat hard to swallow by future generations.

For the scoffers and mockers who believe that Paul is contradicting the author of Hebrews by going against his words in Hebrews 4:12, let's take a moment to view this passage of Scripture:

> *For the word of God is living and powerful, and sharper than any two-edged sword, piercing even to the division of soul and spirit, and of joints and marrow, and is a discerner of the thoughts and intents of the heart.*

The above Scripture holds true if and only if the mind is not seared with a hot iron. This helps to explain why the un-saved person who hears an anointed message from God can walk away literally unmoved, easily rejecting God's offer for salvation. The word has a profound effect only upon those who are hungry and thirsty for righteousness.

That being said, we live in an era that readily accepts deceit and fabricated messages behind our pulpits. I cannot

26

count the times hearing a preacher preach a dynamic message, saying God had given him that thought for that particular service, knowing that he had preached that message verbatim from a popular book of the day. The competition for excellence has risen to the lying stage in hopes of looking good in the eyes of our audience. All the while, the unconverted and the Church both go without being ministered to.

Time for a Showdown

In all honesty, it is time for a showdown much like the one at Mt. Carmel between Elijah and the prophets of Baal. These false prophets had the ear of King Ahab and were helping to lead Israel into idolatry. Yet, they were pretty much all talk and no action. They were eloquent in their oratory, articulate in every way. They expressed themselves in ways that could move a crowd into a frenzy, but the bottom line was their ministry was powerless. They were only halfway there.

The competition for godly supremacy was simple. Build an altar, and whichever god answered their prayer by consuming the sacrifice with fire, would be determined as the one true God. The prophets of Baal took the lead, but their idea of demonstration left something to be desired. For hours and hours, leaping on the altar, cutting themselves to draw blood, this expressive show of emotion did not bring the desired result. Their ranting and raving became comical, and Elijah began to rattle them with his taunting.

> *So they took the bull which was given them, and they prepared it, and called on the name of Baal from morning even till noon, saying, "O Baal, hear us!" But there was no voice; no one answered. Then they leaped about the altar which they had made. And so it was, at noon, that Elijah mocked them and*

said, "Cry aloud, for he is a god; either he is meditating, or he is busy, or he is on a journey, or perhaps he is sleeping and must be awakened." And when midday was past, they prophesied until the time of the offering of the evening sacrifice. But there was no voice; no one answered, no one paid attention. (1 Kings 18:26-29)

They continued their yapping till the evening sacrifice, to no avail. They finally sat down in utter defeat, giving way to an anointed man of God.

When Elijah emphatically took control of the situation, it did not take him long to convince the crowd that this prophet of God had a lot of experience demonstrating God's power. Check out his resume and you will find that it was he (Elijah) who prophesied a lack of rain for a period of three years. With that sort of anointing working for you, what is there to be afraid of? He proceeded to build an altar and prepared a sacrifice according to the Law of Moses. To demonstrate the confidence and faith he had in his God, he solicited help to pour out four water pots over the sacrifice, not once, not twice, but three times.

It was at this juncture in the Scriptures that Elijah displayed for everyone to see the powerful anointing that God had placed in his life. Listen to this simple prayer:

And it came to pass, at the time of the offering of the evening sacrifice, that Elijah the prophet came near and said, "LORD God of Abraham, Isaac, and Israel, let it be known this day that You are God in Israel and I am Your servant, and that I have done all these things at Your word. Hear me, O LORD, hear me, that this people may know that You are the LORD God, and that You have turned their hearts back to You again." (1 Kings 18:36-37)

It took only a total of 63 words uttered in roughly 24 seconds for the God of heaven to respond with enough fire to totally consume Elijah's sacrifice. What did it take for Elijah to obtain this kind of power and anointing? Is it readily available to anyone in God's kingdom, or is it reserved to a precious few? In asking these questions myself, I came to the conclusion that there is a three-step process that will unlock the doors to unlimited resources of anointing.

The Process to a Powerful Anointing
Separation from the world and unto God is the first step. Second Corinthians 6:17 states: *Therefore come out from among them and be separate, says the Lord. Do not touch what is unclean, and I will receive you.* To be set apart means to be separated for a purpose, literally severed. When I was initiated into the ministry, the term that was used to explain the process was "being set aside to the ministry". There was an understanding that although friends and family would continue to be an integral part of my life, it was equally important to set aside time away from them to grow closer to God. A new lifestyle needed to be created, sacrificing time from my normal routine to accommodate my new responsibilities in God. I have observed among many of my peers that lack of separation. It is so much easier to add ministry to the lists of our accomplishments rather than reinventing ourselves through our separation onto God. If we are willing to take that first step into our new way of life, then the next step will not appear so intimidating to us as we continue to yield our lives unto the Lord.

Consecration unto the Father, the second step, has descended to the level of a "necessary evil" rather than a standard of living. Prayer, fasting, and waiting in His presence has never been man's idea of getting things done efficiently in the kingdom of God. In the fast-paced days that we live in, God's ways are extremely slow and His archaic methods have been slowly replaced by our talents, know-how, and modern technology. We dabble in a minimum of consecration to cover all the bases, making sure that we are not bypassing this particular area in the kingdom of God.

But it has become evident that we have misunderstood the purpose of consecration and its importance as well. We have been taught that as we make sacrifices unto the Lord, it is we who are consecrating ourselves. That is so far from the truth that we need to revisit Leviticus 8:33 to find out where our consecration in reality comes from.

And you shall not go outside the door of the tabernacle of meeting for seven days, until the days of your consecration are ended. For seven days he shall consecrate you.

Believing that we are consecrated by our own efforts is about as absurd as believing we can cleanse ourselves of our own sin. Consecrating our lives is a God thing, predicated on our willingness to humble ourselves in His presence until He completes the job. It is then and only then that the fruit of our sacrifice can be made readily available to us.

When the Lord finishes consecrating us, the benefits that await us are far above what we deserve. A consecrated life results in intimate fellowship with the Master. There is not only a newfound sensation of fulfillment in Him, there is a replenishment of strength to the weary soul, invigorating the spirit to press on with a God-given vitality. If that weren't enough, power and dominion at heightened levels are now at our disposal, wreaking havoc over the enemy. This all comes to fruition when God makes a decision to consecrate us. Our initial fellowship with Him grows to intimate relationship. It is that intimate relationship with our Heavenly Father that brings into motion the power and anointing that we so desperately seek in Him.

What We Truly Lack Today

Two steps in the process of obtaining power and anointing have been discussed. Now it's time to proceed to the last step, which is demonstration. The Apostle Paul invariably knew that demonstration was the secret weapon of his power and anointing. He had no problem admitting his weaknesses because he understood that with a step of faith, he could overcome them with power and anointing made available from his consecrated life.

I was with you in weakness, in fear, and in much trembling. And my speech and my preaching were not with persuasive words of human wisdom, but in demonstration of the Spirit and of power, that your faith should not be in the wisdom of men but in the power of God. (1 Cor 2:3-5)

His honesty helps us conclude that there is more to ministry than preaching. In reality, we're only halfway there.

As an evangelist, my point of view has usually been quite different from those I come in contact with. Having the ability to travel across the United States, Mexico, and Central and South America, I have been able to broaden my horizons with a clearer picture of the state that the Church finds itself in today. I am rapidly approaching the 40-year mark in my serving of the Lord, and I have seen both good and bad come and go. We as ministers have made such great strides and inroads into our maturity process. Our work in the field has brought us great success. For years we had struggled with our dignified ways on the platform. It was not uncommon for us to admonish our congregations

31

to offer more of an effort in their praise and worship, when at the same time we offered little ourselves. We have subsequently changed our ways and our approach to Him in the Spirit, including our level of worship ascending to heaven as a sweet-smelling savor unto Him. There is one thing, though, I believe we have forgotten as we approach Him. As important as it is to minister unto our Master, it is equally important to minister unto His children. It appears to be a strange statement made to those who preach at least a couple of times a week to their congregations. Preaching touches God's people from a distance, whereas signs and wonders will minister to them in a more personal way. Preaching is done generally for their sake, yet unleashing signs and wonders into their lives are the "direct hit" from heaven that they are lacking.

The Good Samaritan

It is somewhat eerie to accept the thought that our ministries parallel the ones that we find in the account of the Good Samaritan. (Luke 10:33-37) In this parable, Jesus told a story of a certain man who made the journey from Jerusalem to Jericho. While on his journey, he was attacked, robbed, and left for dead. A little time later, a priest also making his way to Jericho made a concerted effort to bypass this man in distress by consciously walking across to the other side of the street. In doing so, he had hoped to be far enough away from the situation so as not to have to deal with it. It wasn't much time after this that a Levite also came passing by. He was not as grossly negligent as the priest, in that he at least took a peek at this wounded man, perhaps muttering something to him before he too crossed the street to avoid any more direct confrontation with this stranger who was more dead than alive.

Because none of their constituents would ever know of this indiscretion, their reputations would stay intact. Who could blame them? They were on their way home from a hard day's work. In those days, Jericho was considered the "Palm Springs" of Palestine and their minds were on a little R&R. This line of reasoning would have been absolutely accepted if it weren't for the fact that a Samaritan man journeying to Jericho for the same reason stopped to help. He not only bandaged this stranger's wounds, he took him to a hotel, rented a room, and cared for him the rest of the night. Furthermore, the next morning he talked to the innkeeper, paying him for his trouble and said to him to continue to take care of this stranger. If there was more money to be spent, do it, and when the Samaritan man returned he would repay any more money that had been spent to care for this man.

The one thing that stands out in this story, that the reader should take note of is this. The Samaritan used wine and oil to bandage the wounds, relieving the stranger's pain. In other words, an anointing took place as this Samaritan personally ministered unto him. Our ministries begin and end behind the pulpit. The distance from the platform to the altar is the same distance needed for the Priest and the Levite to cross the street. If that be true, why is it so hard for us to leave our comfort zone behind the pulpit, coming down to the altar where the real need is? If we compare our ministries to that of the Samaritan, we are truly only halfway there.

My words up to this point have been somewhat blunt and unsympathetic to ministers who have not yet expanded their ministries beyond preaching. There is, of course, a line of reasoning for such candid language. Listen to something that happened to me a couple of years ago.

A Hard Lesson Learned

Growing up, I lived next to a particular neighbor for several years. His children were pretty much the same age as my sisters and I. When his youngest daughter, Barbara (not her real name) married, she married a young man the family always seemed to look down on. Everyone took their shots at him one at a time, but being good-natured as he was the verbal bullets bounced off of him like water off a duck's back. Bobby (not his real name) was not as quick on his feet to respond to their abuse, if you know what I mean, so consequently he put up with it. My heart always went out to Bobby, but I never really took the time to talk to him about the Lord.

One day as Bobby came over to his father-in-law's to visit, I noticed that he was limping. When I asked him if he was all right, he responded that it wasn't anything serious, just a little pain in his leg. Within a matter of six months, he went from limping, to the use of a cane, to walking with a walker, then being confined to a wheelchair and finally sent to a rest home. Bobby had been stricken with multiple sclerosis.

Before he physically wore out, I made a feeble attempt to minister unto him, lasting about two minutes tops. One day as he sat on the porch in front of his father-in-law's house, I quickly made a dash to talk to him before his father-in-law found out. His father-in-law was a nonreligious man, bordering on atheism. He wanted no part of God, neither did he give time to anybody who did. Any time you mentioned God in his presence, his response was always rude, crude, with curse words flying in all directions. With this circling in the back of my mind, I gave Bobby the shallowest, uninspired presentation of the Gospel that anybody could give. I then hightailed it out of there, washing my hands of guilt, believing I had complied with my soul-winning responsibilities. Boy, was I sadly mistaken. Bobby died a few weeks later without God, and it was then that I realized I was only halfway there.

Since that time, I've come to understand why many people in despair don't come to us as ministers for help. The scripture written in Psalm 60:11 comes to mind.

Give us help from trouble, for the help of man is useless.

This is a prayer made directly to God. It is very possible that this person making the prayer does not even know God, nor does he comprehend how to get answers from Him. Nevertheless, he makes a meager attempt to find God because he is utterly frustrated with the lack of help he is receiving from the Ministry.

There is a godly call from heaven's portals, admonishing us to fully preach the gospel with signs and wonders attached to our ministries. If we will truly separate ourselves onto God, letting Him consecrate us, we will demonstrate with a powerful anointing. We must be willing to pay the full price for the full Gospel. Anything less means we are only halfway there.

35

CHAPTER 3

Plain Wrapped Anointing *Baby Jesus*

———— ⊱⋅⊰ ————

And this will be the sign to you: You will find a Babe wrapped in swaddling cloths, lying in a manger."   (Luke 2:12)

Plain is not the way that any of us would like to be perceived. Whether we are talking about our looks, the way we dress, how we talk, or where we live, etc. etc. etc., plain is just not acceptable. Why? Because no one wants to lack beauty, or to be considered ordinary in any way, especially if that means reaching the level of ugly. But there is another side of plain that we fail to consider. That other side of plain means we are dealing with something that is pure, clear, and most obvious[1]. In actuality, isn't that the way we would always want our lives? It behooves us not to reject the plain things in life because there just might be a hidden blessing that is not visible to the naked eye. I will never forget an auntie of mine who was notorious for giving expensive gifts for birthdays and at Christmas time. What blew us all away was the fact that these pricey gifts were always wrapped in newspaper. Don't think for a moment that she was not able to afford a more expensive wrapping, because that wasn't the point. She wanted us to understand it wasn't the outside wrapping that made the family desirous of her gifts, but more importantly what was on the inside. If for no other reason, everybody loved receiving gifts from her.

The Tabernacle in the Wilderness

This is the same concept the Lord used when He gave Moses the instructions of how to build a tabernacle in the wilderness. The inside of His house would be gaudy; the outside was to be kept plain and simple. The outer covering was made of black goats' hair. As far as appearance goes, it was nothing to write home about. It was as plain as plain could be. This bizarre-looking, oblong-shaped eyesore was so inconspicuous that the enemies of Israel never imagined that the Hebrews' most sacred building would appear so ordinary.

On the other hand, what went into the constructing of the Holy Place and the Holy of Holies was a completely different story. Beauty, splendor, and magnificence were reserved for this portion of God's meeting place. The colors of royalty blue, scarlet and purple dominated the interior. The veils and curtains that lined the walls were woven with fine cloth, not to be outdone by the pillars overlaid with gold. The interior and its contents were truly a work of art. The wood used for the furniture was the best money could buy[2].

The message was made crystal clear that the palace the presence of the Lord dwelled in was to be the main focus of His people and would be a constant reminder of His majesty and glory. The inside of the tabernacle would take preeminence, with nothing else coming even close. The outside would not hold the same significance. It was constructed in a way that its outer appearance would not compete with the inner court's purpose, that being a place to house the glory of God.

Why God Uses Signs

If our lives were as uncomplicated as the little-used definition of plain, there would not be such a great need for signs. But because the Christian life is founded on faith, a concept that forfeits the control of our lives, God uses an occasional sign to keep us on the right path. These signs have the ability to calm our nerves when making key decisions, thus we have the tendency to become dependent on them. This dependency at times borders on addiction, refusing to move without them. Our trust in signs becomes greater than our trust in the giver of signs, which causes lots of problems in our relationship with the Lord. It is easy to forget that signs were given to guide us, not to dictate or rule over us in any way, shape, or form. These are the bona fide reasons that the Lord had in mind when He decided to use signs in the first place.

In a world that offers a countless number of paths leading us away from God, it is paramount to know that one path will lead us to Him.

Look upon me and be merciful to me, as Your custom is toward those who love Your name. Direct my steps by Your word, and let no iniquity have dominion over me. (Ps 119:132,133)

Once that direction is determined, signs will continue to be given for clarification. When the Jewish nation was given a promise that a coming Messiah would rescue them from captivity, they began to look for signs. Jesus understood that His brethren had such a strong inclination for "sign" gazing that when John's disciples came to inquire if He was the promised Messiah they were looking for, His response was deep rooted in scripture, knowing that the signs written in prophecy would clarify His ministry.

39

Jesus answered and said to them, "Go and tell John the things you have seen and heard: that the blind see, the lame walk, the lepers are cleansed, the deaf hear, the dead are raised, the poor have the gospel preached to them And blessed is he who is not offended because of Me." (Luke 7:22-23)

Anyone well-versed in Old Testament Scripture could admit that the words Jesus spoke that day came right out of the book of Isaiah. With this sign so blatantly clear, it was easy for John to pronounce Jesus the long-awaited Messiah. The last reason why signs are given to us is for an identity. Several hundred years after the prophecy was given that Israel was to await its Savior, every child born was looked at as a possible reigning king. How would the Messiah be identified? A sign, of course, would identify the baby, one that was both clear and unique.

And this will be the sign to you: You will find a Babe wrapped in swaddling cloths, lying in a manger." (Luke 2:12)

The Perfect Sign

The manger Jesus was born in fits the sign of His birth perfectly, in that it was a borrowed room in the neighborhood of Bethlehem. In actuality, it was not the animal-type stall that we are accustomed to seeing in pictures, but rather according to Jewish tradition, a cave hewn out of stone[3].

His humble, modest, down-to-earth beginning would be the pattern formed to follow in His footsteps. In other words, His birth was setting the stage for a plain wrapped anointing, one that was clear, precise, and direct. This anointing in its simplicity would be plain yet powerful, easily attainable by anyone and for everyone.

I had made a statement earlier that plain was not acceptable. The definition of "plain" is pretty much relative, taking into consideration the eye of the beholder. What might be perfect in one's eye is ghastly in another's. That is why there are occasions when people attempt to improve on perfection. If that is not bad enough, there are times when you come across people who are just never satisfied. The wisest man who ever lived, King Solomon, had something to say about this subject in Proverbs 27:20:

...the eyes of man are never satisfied.

I believe that John Henry Ford had this view in mind when his car company adopted the slogan, "Ford has a better idea". It was their moniker for years, intimating that they could top anything put out by the big three car companies in Detroit, if given the opportunity.

This is what capitalism has hung its hat on for so many years, helping the United States ascend to be the number one manufacturing country in the world. It is only till recently that those more ambitious countries, adopting the same philosophy, have taken the top spot away from us. The industrial and technological crowns that we as a nation wore so proudly have also been taken away by the more aggressive nations. Their advancements in these areas have left us eating their dust.

That being said, herein lies the problem in dealing with spiritual matters. You cannot improve on spiritual perfection, especially when trying to apply worldly concepts to spiritual principles.

The Sons of Sceva

The sons of Sceva (Acts 19:13-16) found this out the hard way. These hotshot Jewish exorcists attempted to use the name of Jesus to heighten the appeal of their ministries. For some time, they had observed the Apostle Paul, who had the entire city of Ephesus completely mesmerized by the "unusual miracles" he produced by invoking the name of Jesus. His anointing was plain, simple, and powerful, careful to always give the glory to God.

Once they were satisfied that they had a handle on releasing this new power, they copied the same words Paul used to cast out a demon. They had no authority to use the name, much less use it for their vainglory. They were then exposed by the evil spirits and were humiliated when stripped of their clothes, being left naked.

The same principle rings true even when those in authority candy coat the name of Jesus with worldly styles, fashions, techniques, and methods. These high-flying ministries are bathed in Madison Avenue technique with a sprinkling of Hollywood glamour. Their motives may be pure but the results are tainted. The numbers that are accumulated by winning the lost are incredible, yet these people are won to their magnetic personalities and not necessarily to God.

The Parable of the Sower

We can equate this form of "winning souls to God" to the Parable of the Sower:

> But he who received the seed on stony places, this is he who hears the word and immediately receives it with joy; yet he has no root in himself, but endures only for a while. For when tribulation or persecution arises because of the word, immediately he stumbles. (Matt 13:20-21)

There are numerous converts being swept off of their feet by captivating and compelling ministries. They receive their salvation with gladness and unspeakable joy, yet their root is founded more on charisma, flowery messages, and seeker-friendly lessons than in truth. They are never quite

Careful to always give the glory to God.

primed for the spiritual warfare that they will be engaged in an overwhelming fashion, on terms that are not fair to the unprepared. Matthew 13:21 then documents the consequences of these mistakes ...*yet he has no root in himself, but endures only for a while. For when tribulation or persecution arises because of the word, immediately he stumbles.*

There are far too many people who have come to Christ for the wrong reasons, and when they slip out the back door because of their inability to handle tough times, we are left frustrated, trying to figure out where we went wrong. The fact of the matter is this: the simple and plain signs of a successful Christian life are being overshadowed by more radiant signs covering God's truth.

Then Jesus said to His disciples, "If anyone desires to come after Me, let him deny himself, and take up his cross, and follow Me. For whoever desires to save his life will lose it, but whoever loses his life for My sake will find it." (Matt 16:24-25)

A Lost Art

Denial, as we have known it in the past, is a concept that has been erased from our vocabulary now for some time. It has been replaced by prosperity doctrines that help us to receive our blessings at the moment we can "name it and claim it". Following God by denying oneself and picking up a heavy, splinter-filled cross is so "old school." In today's society, there is no longer a need to venture out into the dark when there are well lit signs, ones that are rational, logical, and reasonable, leading us to roads that are well-traveled. True as this may be, broad, well-traveled roads do not always lead to a better place.

"Enter by the narrow gate; for wide is the gate and broad is the way that leads to destruction, and there

are many who go in by it. Because narrow is the gate and difficult is the way which leads to life, and there are few who find it. (Matt 7:13-14)

Don't always pay attention to the signs that lead you to an easier life. The illogical, nonsensical, difficult way will most times lead to a better way of life. Why? Because it's God's way!

The life the Apostle Paul lived surely strengthens this argument for denial. His plain and simple life did in fact provide for him a powerful anointing, but it did come at a great price. In a conversation he was not privy to, the Lord specifically told Ananias to minister unto this new convert, also alluding to the fact that Paul would suffer greatly for His kingdom.

But the Lord said to him, "Go, for he is a chosen vessel of Mine to bear My name before Gentiles, kings, and the children of Israel. For I will show him how many things he must suffer for My name's sake." (Acts 9:15-16)

Why, because he was a chosen vessel, with a special mission, to honor a special God. The Lord would personally assure him of his calling through signs and wonders. The confirmation of this would come in the form of fellowship with God through suffering.

Paul/Saul

Simplify, Simplify, Simplify

When Paul came to the Lord as Saul, his life needed simplifying. To identify with Christ, his life needed to be made plainer. Unlike the Lord, the Apostle Paul did not have humble beginnings.

If anyone else thinks he may have confidence in the flesh, I more so: circumcised the eighth day, of the

my life needed simplifying. Paul - needed to be made plainer

stock of Israel, of the tribe of Benjamin, a Hebrew of the Hebrews; concerning the law, a Pharisee; concerning zeal, persecuting the church; concerning the righteousness which is in the law, blameless. (Phil 3:4-6)

He was a pretty proud fellow, if I do say so myself. His affluent, highly respected, and successful life before Christ was filled with pride. It was vital to his ministry to strip him of all the unnecessary baggage that would hinder his calling before God.

When he was able to grasp the enormity of his assignment, he willingly humbled himself to a life of plain and simple. No bells and whistles, no fanfare, no hoopla. He had no entourage bowing to his every whim or a manager preceding him, booking his meetings in the largest arenas of the day. There were no publicity agents announcing his visits through the media. He knew his place and understood his mission. He then voluntarily accepted the difficult times that came his way, knowing that it was the Master's sign to him that he was in the perfect will of God. He was never embarrassed by his suffering, with the Scriptures documenting every beating, thrashing, and trouncing endured for the Gospel's sake.

...in labors more abundant, in stripes above measure, in prisons more frequently, in deaths often. From the Jews five times I received forty stripes minus one. Three times I was beaten with rods; once I was stoned; three times I was shipwrecked; a night and a day I have been in the deep; in journeys often, in perils of waters, in perils of robbers, in perils of my own countrymen, in perils of the Gentiles, in perils in the city, in perils in the wilderness, in perils in the sea, in perils among false brethren; in weariness and toil, in

45

sleeplessness often, in hunger and thirst, in fastings often, in cold and nakedness besides the other things, what comes upon me daily: my deep concern for all the churches. (2 Cor 11:23-28)

He came to the simple conclusion that nothing could separate him from the love of Christ. His words strongly verified this.

Who shall separate us from the love of Christ? Shall tribulation, or distress, or persecution, or famine, or nakedness, or peril, or sword? As it is written: "For Your sake we are killed all day long; we are accounted as sheep for the slaughter." Yet in all these things we are more than conquerors through Him who loved us. For I am persuaded that neither death nor life, nor angels nor principalities nor powers, nor things present nor things to come, nor height nor depth, nor any other created thing, shall be able to separate us from the love of God which is in Christ Jesus our Lord. (Rom 8:35-39)

Because he kept his life plain and simple, his anointing stayed pure, clear, and powerful. His successful life of signs, wonders and miracles never enticed him to steal the glory from God. For this reason, he was able to end his life with honor.

Ending a Life with Honor

For I am already being poured out as a drink offering, and the time of my departure is at hand. I have fought the good fight, I have finished the race, I have kept the faith. (2 Tim 4:6-7)

These are the words of a grizzly veteran schooled in the art of suffering. Down through the years, his spectacular accomplishments have inspired others to follow in his footsteps. But the one thing that stands out about his life is the unique fellowship that he had with God. Plain and simple, it was a fellowship that was founded and embellished on suffering.

> *Yet indeed I also count all things loss for the excellence of the knowledge of Christ Jesus my Lord, for whom I have suffered the loss of all things, and count them as rubbish, that I may gain Christ and be found in Him, not having my own righteousness, which is from the law, but that which is through faith in Christ, the righteousness which is from God by faith; that I may know Him and the power of His resurrection, and the fellowship of His sufferings, being conformed to His death...*
>
> (Phil 3:8-10).

In the two last references written above, the apostle makes the attempt to connect himself with Christ's death. The passage in Philippians is much more direct than his writings in 2 Timothy. It is in the book of Timothy that he references a drink offering in the Old Testament to attach himself to the death of Christ.

Connecting to Christ's Death

The drink offerings, more commonly known as libations, were established in the patriarchal period and accompanied many of the sacrifices (Exodus 29:40). These sacrifices included all free will offerings, the continual burnt sacrifice, Sabbaths, and other established feasts (Num. 28:14-31; 29:6-39). Oil and wine, used separately or as a mixture, constituted the libation. It is the oil in this process that we would like to pay close attention to.

Oil used for these sacrifices, for all intents and purposes, was the purest, most wholesome, uncorrupted and cleanest oil in the entire world. In chapter 1, I took the time to explain the painstaking process to develop the sanctuary oil used for sacrifices, so we will not belabor the point. What I will say is this: the purity of this oil was second to none. Being the expert in Old Testament law that he was, Paul had the total assurance that the oil (his anointing) he was offering unto the Lord in his death was of the highest quality. It wasn't tainted, polluted, or contaminated. It was just plain and simple. His beginnings may have not been humble like his Master's; nevertheless, his death truly did emulate the death of Christ. Only his Roman citizenship exempted him from torture and crucifixion, or he would have gladly followed in the Lord's footsteps[4].

There is one last sign that bookmarks the position taken in this chapter that I would like to discuss. "Plain and simple" is the emblem that symbolized the life of Christ from his birth. He never strayed, neither did He want to. When men were drawn to His ministry, wanting to be a part of something big, He had to admit to them there was not much glamour in this.

> Then a certain scribe came and said to Him, "Teacher, I will follow You wherever You go." And Jesus said to him, "Foxes have holes and birds of the air have nests, but the Son of Man has nowhere to lay His head." (Matt 8:19-20)

There were times that a lack of money appeared to be an issue. Time and time again He would use His anointing, producing miracles so that the hungry might be fed or in one case pay His taxes.

> When they had come to Capernaum, those who received the temple tax came to Peter and said, "Does your Teacher not pay the temple tax?" He

said, "Yes."..... Jesus said to him ...Nevertheless, lest we offend them, go to the sea, cast in a hook, and take the fish that comes up first. And when you have opened its mouth, you will find a piece of money; take that and give it to them for Me and you." as Temple Tax (Matt 17:24-27)

Now seriously, is this the way to run a kingdom? Couldn't Jesus have chosen a better, more elaborate system to draw people unto Him? Undoubtedly He could have; nonetheless, the signs He chose to use were kept plain and simple even in His death.

Putting It All Together

We have finally come to the point in this chapter where we connect all the dots to see how the death of Jesus parallels with His birth.

Then he bought fine linen, took Him down, and wrapped Him in the linen. And he laid Him in a tomb which had been hewn out of the rock, and rolled a stone against the door of the tomb.
(Mark 15:46)

The fine linen, i.e., grave clothes that were used to wrap Him immediately after His death, were similar to the swaddling clothes used at birth[5]. This type of linen was plain and simple, yet elegant enough to be used for the veil in Solomon's Temple, embroidered by the skill of the Tyrian craftsman (2 Chron. 3:14). His tomb was hewn out of a rock just like the manger. In other words, He died exactly the way He came into this world, plain and simple. It was a sign left to us and to future generations that a plain wrapped anointing was good enough for Him. From His humble beginning to an unpretentious start to His ministry,

He never deviated from the plan. His death would be no different. His last words were plain and simple:

> *He said, "It is finished!" And bowing His head, He gave up His spirit*   (John 19:30)

His plain wrapped anointing from beginning to end brought us the salvation that only He could provide. Thank God for the plain and simple.

End Notes

[1] Webster's Dictionary, definition of plain

[2] International Standard Bible Encyclopedia, Tabernacle

[3] Fausset's Bible Dictionary, Manger

[4] International Standard Bible Encyclopedia, Citizenship

[5] Strong's Dictionary, NT: 4616 (*sindon*)

CHAPTER 4

Used or Abused?

"Not everyone who says to Me, 'Lord, Lord,' shall enter the kingdom of heaven, but he who does the will of My Father in heaven. Many will say to Me in that day, 'Lord, Lord, have we not prophesied in Your name, cast out demons in Your name, and done many wonders in Your name?' And then I will declare to them, 'I never knew you; depart from Me, you who practice lawlessness!' (Matt 7:21-23)

These three verses in the seventh chapter of Matthew have always been fascinating to me because of the great Judgment Day surprise that has caught many Christians unawares. While those in line are waiting for the "fruit of their labor," it is appalling to them that the Lord has not recognized them one bit. The shock is apparent when they come to the realization that all the hard work and sacrifice has been in vain. An even greater slap in the face must be tolerated because the Lord of glory doesn't recognize who they are. Adding insult to injury, the powerful signs, wonders, and miracles produced throughout their lifetime in ministry are reduced to the definition of sin. The dagger to the heart comes when the Lord refuses to have anything to do with them.

How did it ever come to this? What exactly went wrong, where in the journey to find the will of God did they take a wrong turn? The answer to these questions is found in verse 21. The rewards of heaven are reserved solely for those who do the will of the Father, and evidently this was not the case in the lives of those who have been rejected.

A Burning Question

About this time, there should be a burning question in your soul about this situation that does not make any sense. How could prophesying in God's name, casting out demons, and doing wonderful works fall under the category of iniquity? Since when are all of these things not considered in the will of God? Let's examine this dilemma a little closer.

There is a fine line between doing the will of God and allowing our own will to take precedence. Obtaining good results are not good enough to make God overlook our disobedience. Just because an undertaking is successful and thriving at the moment, does not necessarily mean that God has been in it from its inception. Our ignorance in such matters is not an excuse to bypass His will.

> *If anyone wills to do His will, he shall know concerning the doctrine, whether it is from God...He who speaks from himself seeks his own glory; but He who seeks the glory of the One who sent Him is true, and no unrighteousness is in Him*
> (John 7:17-18)

If we continue to let our will override His, then it is our glory that is being sought, not His. If we are honestly seeking the face of God to know His will, He will show us what is right. His doctrine cannot be compromised whether in the area of salvation, regeneration, or holiness. His way is the only way.

The consequences of our carelessness far outweigh the risks we take to minister out of the will of God. I am sure that an eternity that does not include heaven is not what we had in mind when we meditate on our final resting place. We must not let the greatest opportunity to serve the Master go to waste on our own indulgences.

This Just Doesn't Sound Right

The hardest thing to swallow in accepting what is being written is the fact that there is a possibility God will continue to honor our efforts, even when we're out of His will, to manipulate an outcome. Manipulation in the kingdom of God doesn't sound Christian. True, but before you run me off as a false prophet, give me an opportunity to explain.

When at times God chooses to use willful, headstrong people to do a particular work, He will honor His word but not necessarily honor them. There is one reason and only one reason why God would stoop to such a level to answer petitions being brought before His throne. He does it for the sake of the sheep, His children who are in desperate need of help. We know that the scriptures compare God's children to sheep. Sheep have to be led to eat and drink. They must depend on others for their shelter. It goes without saying if they are hurt in any way, they are totally dependent on someone else to bring them back to health. Knowing this, God bends over backwards to make sure His sheep are well taken care of, and if manipulation is in order, so be it. I actually can prove this through the scriptures.

Then the LORD spoke to Moses, saying, "Take the rod; you and your brother Aaron gather the congregation together. Speak to the rock before their eyes, and it will yield its water; thus you shall bring water for them out of the rock, and give drink to the congregation and their animals." So Moses took the rod from before the LORD as He commanded him. And Moses and Aaron gathered the assembly together before the rock; and he said to them, "Hear now, you rebels! Must we bring water for you out of this rock?" Then Moses lifted his hand and struck the rock twice with his rod; and water came out abundantly, and the congregation and their animals drank. Then the LORD spoke to Moses and Aaron, "Because you did not believe Me, to hallow Me in the eyes of the children of Israel, therefore you shall not bring this assembly into the land which I have given them." (Num 20:7-12)

Moses had to deal with a rebellious bunch that was constantly griping about something. In this particular case, there was a need for water. It was the second time in their journey through the wilderness that their water supply had gone dry. You would think that after seeing God do a great miracle to supply them the water they needed once before, they would not be stressing so much this time. We have to remember that we're talking about the children of Israel here. This assortment of carnal, backbiting, impatient Hebrews was accustomed to pushing their leaders' tolerance to the limit.

As Moses prepared himself to receive this blessing from God, I can only imagine what was going through his mind. Leading a group of unappreciative, grumbling people can quickly wear out even the strongest of men. Could it be that his lingering to complete the job was a sign that he had mentally given up on these crazy protesters? Who knows what was going on in his mind as he contemplated the assignment set before him? God had given him specific instructions that this time around, the miracle would be produced by speaking to the rock instead of hitting it with his rod. Now the Scriptures do not say this, so what I'm about to write is only speculation. I would not put it past them to hear taunting coming Moses' way, challenging him to hit the rock with his rod.

"Hey Moses," they yelled in unison. "What are you waiting for, man?"

"Hit the rock already and get it over with, we're dying of thirst!"

This meek, mild-mannered man uncharacteristically lost his temper, yielding to their taunts, and struck the rock. Although this was not done according to plan, God responded anyway with water gushing all over the place. Their faith was restored both in God and in Moses, and in their eyes Moses was the man. not God,

Disobedience Has Its Consequences

There were consequences to Moses' disobedience that appeared harsher than what was warranted. The children of Israel never had a clue that God was distraught with His leader. They figured because God had answered their need through him, he must have been on good terms with the Lord. The problem was, that wasn't necessarily the case. The result of Moses not obeying God's instructions forced the Lord to banish him from entering into the Promised Land.

Is it really possible for Christians to have an anointing or gifts while ministering and still be out of the will of God? Consider this scripture that was written to us in the book of James 3:1,2:

> *My brethren, let not many of you become teachers, knowing that we shall receive a stricter judgment. For we all stumble in many things.*

The teacher label discussed in this scripture must readily include those in any type of ministry. As we all know, whether we are preachers, choir directors, ushers or the like, teaching is at the foundation of every ministry. Because we are apt to stumble in many things, we therefore must consider that there are blind spots and presumptuous sins in our lives as well.

> *Who can understand his errors? Cleanse me from secret faults. Keep back your servant also from presumptuous sins; Let them not have dominion over me. Then I shall be blameless, and I shall be innocent of great transgression. Let the words of my mouth and the meditation of my heart be acceptable in Your sight,* (Ps 19:12-14)

Believing that the Lord would not judge those in ministry more harshly truly falls under a category of arrogant and condescending. It is the same type of arrogance God will display on judgment day when He rejects our works as iniquity. He ends up manipulating our ministries for the sake of the sheep and we end up with a Judgment Day surprise.

What About Anointing?
Doesn't a powerful anointing prove that God's hand is upon them, solidifying His approval? Not really. In God's economy, character, not anointing, is number one on His priority list. Success without character will always end in disaster, that's why the Lord invests so much time in us to build our character to a level of hope. Paul said as much to the Romans in Chapter 5, verses 3-5:

> *And not only that, but we also glory in tribulations, knowing that tribulation produces perseverance; and perseverance, character; and character, hope. Now hope does not disappoint, because the love of*

God has been poured out in our hearts by the Holy Spirit who was given to us.

Character not only yields to hope, but it allows us to see ourselves in the way we really are. Being alone away from the crowds truly exposes our character. What we are when we are alone is what God sees and judges. Although we strive without reservation to seek His gifts of the Spirit, He would rather we take the time to bear the fruit of that same Spirit.

It is the fruit of the Spirit that God adds to our lives for the building of our character. Whether the speaking gifts, the knowing gifts, or the power gifts are in operation, if there is not a corresponding fruit of the Spirit balancing out those gifts, your life will not be complete. Here is a list of the gifts of the Spirit with their corresponding fruit[1]:

The Speaking Gifts

Tongues	Faith
Interpretation	Temperance
Prophecy	Joy

The Knowing Gifts

Word of Knowledge	Gentleness
Wisdom	Peace
Discerning of Spirits	Long-suffering

The Power Gifts

Faith	Meekness
Gifts of Healing	Love
Working of Miracles	Goodness

Because operating in the gifts of the Spirit is far more easily attainable by impartation and more dynamic in nature, they are preferred over the fruit of the Spirit. The fruit of the Spirit, on the other hand, takes time to develop. Cultivating a crop has always been a time-consuming effort, yet when the harvest time comes and the farmer reaps what he has sown, there is no greater satisfaction one feels when he gets to enjoy the "fruit of his labor."

There are no 90-day wonders in the Lord, although gifted people seem to pop up out of nowhere to do the incredible. If those gifts are not balanced out by a corresponding fruit, then the old adage, "easy come, easy go," will come into play and that promising ministry appearing so invincible will fall by the wayside and die.

King Saul's Anointing

Where was King Saul's anointing when he needed it most? This tall, handsome, first king of Israel lost his composure when the ladies of the city rejoiced after victory in battle, singing this song: ~~to David~~

> *Now it had happened as they were coming home, when David was returning from the slaughter of the Philistine, that the women had come out of all the cities of Israel, singing and dancing, to meet King Saul, with tambourines with joy, and with musical instruments. So the women sang, as they danced, and said: "Saul has slain his thousands, and David his ten thousands."* (1 Sam 18:6-7)

Should not the king have reacted in a more mature and confident manner? After all, he was God's anointed, with all of heaven backing him up. The problem was this: Saul never had the opportunity to cultivate his character. From one day to the next, he went from a nobody to the king of the mightiest country in the entire world. No bumps or bruises, nor dangerous potholes to avoid, just smooth sailing all the way to the throne room. His insecurities (character faults) caused him to react like a heathen.

How David's Character Was Formed

That was not the case with King David. After he was anointed by Samuel to take the throne after Saul, there was a five-year waiting period until that throne was vacated. The training for that position actually began many years prior to that. David learned obedience caring for his sheep, very much the same way the Lord Himself learned obedience in the wilderness. Being alone in the field allowed David precious time to form habits of worship and praise. These habits benefited him in the future as he walked with God. His faith also had an opportunity to grow when great tests of valor presented themselves. The challenges grew in intensity, beginning with the killing of a lion and then a bear. He graduated to the challenge of a lifetime. The Philistine giant Goliath had dared anyone to fight him one-on-one. Of course David was not about to back down to this uncircumcised heathen. With one shot of his sling, he downed public enemy number one and then chopped off his head.

David's greatest challenge came after he was anointed to take Saul's place as the next king of Israel. Although King Saul was completely backslidden and out of the will of God, it still did not give David the right to oust the king before the rightful time. His integrity rose to the surface when one of his mighty men suggested the murder of King Saul.

Then Abishai said to David, "God has delivered your enemy into your hand this day. Now therefore, please, let me strike him at once with the spear, right to the earth; and I will not have to strike him a second time!" But David said to Abishai, "Do not destroy him; for who can stretch out his hand against the LORD's anointed, and be guiltless?"

(1 Sam 26:8-9)

59

With his training complete and his character in order, David was now ready to ascend to the throne.

Anointed Yet Unbalanced

King Saul did not have the same luxury. He was pressed into his reign without any character building whatsoever. His on-the-job training was not sufficient to overcome any character flaws. Now years later, with an unstable psyche that controlled his every move, he made an unwise decision that would eventually cost him his life. He decided to protect his throne. He failed to realize that if God had placed him as king of Israel, only God could replace him. There was no need to worry about being overtaken, because God ultimately and unequivocally had his back. One must come to the realization that if a throne, or in our case a ministry, has to be protected, maybe God didn't put us there in the first place.

His attempts on David's life fell short countless of times, increasing his frustration and aggravation. When the pressure became too great to handle, in a moment of weakness on the battlefield, he committed suicide. He was truly anointed yet totally unbalanced. His anointing could not protect him in his greatest time of need.

I think the saddest part about being used by God and/or being manipulated for the sake of the sheep is that in the process of it all, we really don't get to know Him any better. We may be working for Him, nevertheless we never become *"laborers together with Him."* (1 Cor. 3: 9) Unlike Abraham, who ascended to the level of "friend," we are nothing more than hired guns, knowing about Him but not really knowing Him. But do you want to know what's even worse? He (God) doesn't know us either.

We don't come anywhere near the relationship that the Apostle Paul had with our Lord. As was mentioned in the last chapter, Paul's relationship with God was predicated on his willingness to fellowship with the Lord in his suffering.

Today as the Lord searches for others with that same willingness, there are very few who will take on that challenge.

Holy Impostors

Not knowing Him as He really is hurts us in so many ways. We presume a role that gives the definition of God's anointed a whole new meaning. We now begin to take on the role of impostors:

> *But evil men and impostors will grow worse and worse, deceiving and being deceived* (2 Tim 3:13)

When impostors infiltrate our ranks, their influence has such a great impact on the brethren that living for God becomes very stressful. This is how the Apostle Paul describes them when he writes to Timothy:

> *But know this, that in the last days perilous times will come: For men will be lovers of themselves, lovers of money, boasters, proud, blasphemers, disobedient to parents, unthankful, unholy, unloving, unforgiving, slanderers, without self-control, brutal, despisers of good, traitors, headstrong, haughty, lovers of pleasure rather than lovers of God, having a form of godliness but denying its power. And from such people turn away!*
> (2 Tim 3:1-5)

The Scriptures above do not appear to follow the script that has been adopted for this chapter until we read, *having a form of godliness but denying the power.* Imagine that! This list that documents all that is wrong with the world today is in actuality filled with people donning a religious Spirit and who are anointed. To put it lightly, in the perilous times that we live in today, the enemy we face comes from within not from the outside, working from the guise of deceit.

These anointed impostors are dominating congregations with reckless abandon. They are on the loose with impeccable credentials that make them difficult to refute. Their ability to sway people with their persuasive oratory causes divisions. They will not submit themselves to authority, yet will rant and rave when their words are not taken as gospel. This out-of-control, haughty image of themselves is shrouded by a false humility, one that makes it nearly impossible to unmask. Unfortunately, this is the condition in which we will find the Church in the last days. In pondering our plight, the thing that frightens me the most is how easy it is to fall into this trap. I say this because there have been times in the past when God has had to shake me up to help me see that my motives weren't right.

A Holy Defiance

On more than one occasion, I have stepped up to the pulpit to preach, when at the last moment God has asked me to change my message. Feeling that what I had initially chosen was in actuality the will of God in the first place, there really wasn't any need to make this change He was requesting. It had gotten even worse when, at the time of the altar call, He had asked me to focus on people receiving the Holy Ghost when I of course preferred praying for the sick. What baffles me to this day is how, when I rejected His will, He was still so accommodating when I invoked His name. When the service was finally over and He had miraculously moved throughout the entire congregation, they unknowingly believed that I had complied with the will of God. They thanked me with open arms, begging me to come back so that God could do it again. I knew without a shadow of a doubt that when I returned to my hotel room, God and I were going to have a little talk. He would, like

He had in times past, ask me why I was defiant to Him. What could you say to God that could justify your disobedience to Him? Nothing really, I guess. I have appealed to His mercy in times past and am thankful that my folly was covered under His blood. All I can say about what I have written is that if on judgment day the Lord turned to me, saying, *"Depart from me ye worker of iniquity,"* it would be the saddest day of my life. I look back now on all of the suffering that I've had to endure, the losses ever so painful. There were so many sleepless nights finally crying myself to sleep, coupled with the endless hours of anxiety because my life was in disarray. This anxiety was not easily dismissed because it was part of God's plan to mold my character into the image of Christ. Tolerating the incredible discomfort that arose when friends turned their back on me was one of the worst. Dealing with these unexplainable nightmares in complete solitude was enough to drive a man crazy. Yet, in the back of my mind, all of this suffering would be worth it in the end, receiving an eternal blessing that would be greater than what I had deserved. That, in and of itself, gave me the courage to press on. Now then, if I had to stand on judgment day having to accept that it was all in vain and I had been manipulated, there would be no words that could explain the sorrow I would feel. In that moment, despair does not even begin to illustrate the feeling of hopelessness that would be my companion for all eternity.

I will ask you one more question before I close this chapter. Think deeply before you respond. In your heart of hearts, are you really being used of God? No, really. Are you truly being used of God, or are you being abused? Think about it!

End Notes
[1]   Arcovio, The Way of the Eagle

CHAPTER 5

Counterfeit Anointing

And I, if I am lifted up from the earth/will draw all peoples to Myself." (John 12:32)

I have always been fascinated by counterfeiters and the items they produce. These imitations of pricey merchandise have been manufactured with the intent to deceive. The casual observer will not be able to tell the difference, because if that counterfeiter is worth his weight in salt, his falsified product will look exactly like the original. Whatever you call it bogus, fake, false, forged, unauthentic, phony, or sham this counterfeit merchandise sure does look like the real thing.

When God created us men, He goofed when He didn't put in the same internal alarm that He gave to women. You know what I'm talking about; the alarm that goes off when something fake is being passed off as an original. We are still at a disadvantage when it comes to these things, and consequently I learn a lot when I go shopping with my girls. They can spot a counterfeit a mile away without even comparing prices. That eagle eye and that extra sense are so sensitive that nothing gets past them. I, on the other hand, am the typical man who gets duped into buying a product that looks eerily similar to what I have been sent to the store to buy.

Never send a man alone to buy children's diapers, the results could prove somewhat disastrous. Because a man does not include the fine details of shopping in his repertoire, all he remembers about the diapers he is to buy is that they come in a big red box. When he finally arrives at the store, confident that he can do this successfully, the shock he must overcome looking at three different manufacturers of diapers in red boxes is overwhelming.

Satan's Intentions

It is with the same intentions to mislead that Satan attacks God's children. The effort to deceive is an all-encompassing, no holds barred, fight to the finish. Because eternity is held in the balance, it is a "Battle Royale" for the soul. Be it as it may, this battle has gone on since the beginning of time and we have been duly warned that the master counterfeiter, Satan, would attempt the same in our lives.

> *I marvel that you are turning away so soon from Him who called you in the grace of Christ, to a different gospel, which is not another; but there are some who trouble you and want to pervert the gospel of Christ.* (Gal 1:6-7)

King Rehoboam's Mistake

The biggest mistake initially that King Rehoboam made while assuming the throne of Judah was letting his father's (Solomon) bad example influence him adversely and allowing his mother's idolatry to alter his worship habits. His vain imaginations changed God's glory into an image that was fashioned after all of the abominations of the nations the Lord had cast out before the children of Israel. He began to build sacred pillars and wooden images on every high hill and under every green tree. He placed God's name (Jehovah) on these other idols and continued to worship. It never dawned on him that he was offending his maker so much so that the sins of Judah were not only greater in number, but in depravity as well. His idolatry led the people to vile affections (i.e., homosexuality) that were blatantly visible throughout the kingdom. The same sins that brought judgment upon the nations Judah had defeated became the same sins that brought judgment upon Rehoboam's kingdom. The evil done in the Lord's sight had provoked His jealousy enough to finally turn His back on His own people. Their unrestrained sin weakened them enough to be overtaken by Egypt, who ransacked Jerusalem's riches.

> *It happened in the fifth year of King Rehoboam that Shishak king of Egypt came up against Jerusalem. And he took away the treasures of the house of the LORD and the treasures of the king's house; he took away everything. He also took away all the gold shields which Solomon had made.*
>
> (1 Kings 14:25, 26)

The golden shields made by Solomon, one of Judah's most prized possessions, were taken at this time. They were more ornamental in nature than weapons of war and were brought out in public every once in a while, usually to flaunt Judah's supremacy in the world. Because they could not be easily replaced, Rehoboam decided to put in their place a less expensive counterfeit. The new shields would be made of bronze. Although bronze was considered a precious metal itself, it could never be mistaken for the most precious metal of all, gold. Yet the king did not think twice about replacing the shields with an inferior replica, because by this time in his reign everything that was sacred to God had already been replaced one way or another.

The golden shields had represented the "truth of God" (Ps 91:4), a truth that could not be modified or changed. The truth of God is nonnegotiable and must be left as is, or one must suffer the consequences. This surprising switch only goes to prove how far Rehoboam's judgment had fallen, to the level of being corrupt. Replacing the original would eventually produce a curse, causing him to die an early death.

> *Thus says the LORD God of Israel:* "*Cursed is the man who does not obey the words of this covenant which I commanded your fathers in the day I brought them out of the land of Egypt, from the iron furnace, saying, 'Obey My voice, and do according to all that I command you; so shall you be My people, and I will be your God,'*   (Jer 11:3-4)

Although these words of Jeremiah were written in the future, after the death of Rehoboam, the actual commandment was given to Moses to be applied to the children of Israel and their future generations. This same practice had to be put into play in the life of Moses and the assignment given him to lead the children of Israel out of Egypt.

A Classic Confrontation

The confrontation that Moses had versus the Egyptian magicians was classic. With a sleight of hand that appeared to be real, they attempted to duplicate the miracles of God. Using the state-of-the-art magic common to those times, they attempted to masquerade their trade as if it were a true anointing from God. Just like Moses, they too were able to turn rods into snakes, water into blood, and produced frogs out of nowhere. Their counterfeit anointing was enough to convince Pharaoh that his magicians were on a par with God's finest. The plagues that Egypt experienced, supposedly by the hand of God, were nothing more than magic tricks that could be duplicated by Pharaoh's men.

After three plagues, the Lord made a point that could not be ignored. For the first time in their confrontation with Moses, the Egyptian magicians could not duplicate God's miracles and were restrained by His power. To add to their humiliation, the Lord destroyed all that they held sacred. The Nile, one of their most revered gods, was polluted and their temples of worship were desecrated by frogs. As they tried to remedy the situation to no avail, they finally had to admit that their powers were helpless before the one and true God, Jehovah.

From the fourth plague on, the Lord made a statement to Pharaoh, ensuring that the king knew exactly where the plagues were being initiated from. Until Pharaoh was willing to let the children of Israel leave Egypt, whatever plagues came next would be experienced only by Egyptians. The Lord would protect His people from any further suffering.

> *And in that day I will set apart the land of Goshen, in which My people dwell, that no swarms of flies shall be there, in order that you may know that I am the LORD in the midst of the land. I will make a difference between My people and your people. Tomorrow this sign shall be."* (Ex 8:22-23)

This did not move Pharaoh. With pride rearing its ugly head, he refused to give God glory and release the Israelites.

The Lord then was forced to tighten the grip and the plagues continued in number and in intensity. The fifth plague[1] sent a pestilence for a period of time that guaranteed the death of one of Egypt's most sacred animals, the cow. The same gods they had prayed to for help had been rendered helpless by death.

The Plagues Intensify

The sixth plague[2] began to make things personal in that now the bodies of all Egyptians, including the king, would be attacked by boils. These boils would eventually burst in sores that were very painful. You would think by now Pharaoh would have had a change of heart. Not!

Pharaoh's unwillingness to humble himself brought on plague number seven[3], one that brought with it loss of life. Hail was accompanied by thunder and lightning and it wiped out anything and everything in its path, including humans, plants, and animals. Because of the severity of this plague, the Egyptians were forewarned, and even then Pharaoh did not budge.

Plagues eight[4] and nine[5] entered into the picture, bringing blindness to Egypt in different ways. The locusts that the Lord sent were so many in numbers the Egyptians could not see their own hands, much less breathe, as these insects destroyed everything in their path. An even greater blindness fell upon the land when God blotted out the sun in darkness. This was the ultimate insult to the Egyptians because the sun, their greatest god, was being dominated by Jehovah[6]. This blindness was God's way to set up the Egyptians and Pharaoh to experience the mother of all plagues. Considering that the Lord would not bring a curse upon anyone until they were completely blind, He gave Pharaoh one more opportunity to repent. That opportunity was not taken advantage of.

The final plague, the death to the firstborn, was the most heart-wrenching plague experienced by Egypt.

And it came to pass at midnight that the LORD struck all the firstborn in the land of Egypt, from the firstborn of Pharaoh who sat on his throne to the firstborn of the captive who was in the dungeon, and all the firstborn of livestock. So Pharaoh rose in the night, he, all his servants, and all the

*Egyptians; and there was a great cry in Egypt, for
there was not a house where there was not one
dead.*   (Ex 12:29-30)

Words could not express the pain an entire nation was
forced to endure. Cries of despair and uncontrolled shrieks
of misery could be heard throughout the darkened streets of
Egypt. Everywhere you looked there was agony,
desolation, anguish, and gloom. The unexplained grief
could not be comforted. It was the act that finally brought
Pharaoh to his knees, admitting that Jehovah was the one
and only true God.

What makes a man who has been living a counterfeit
life, serving a counterfeit god, come to the realization that
he has been living a lie? In Pharaoh's case, as he observed
Moses throughout the entire ordeal, there was one thing
constant in the life of the Hebrew leader. Whether in defeat,
despair, disappointment, ridicule, frustration, or confusion,
Jehovah was his main focus. Moses had learned no matter
what the situation he found himself in, if he took the time
to lift up the name of his God, it would draw all men unto
Him.

*And I, if I am lifted up from the earth, will draw all
peoples to Myself."*   (John 12:32)

Moses dealt with his problems by either lifting up his
rod or lifting up the name of his God. God's provision
could not to be denied, if and when His people called out
His name. As simplistic as it sounded, it could never be
invalidated even after Pharaoh, time and time again,
watched the hand of God perform the impossible. If he had
only denounced his magicians as counterfeiters and at the
same time accepted Jehovah as the one true God, the
history books would have recorded a more positive
outcome for him and his nation.

71

How Jesus Dealt with Counterfeiters

Sadly to say, Jesus encountered counterfeit people all the time. One of the reasons why He spoke in parables was to weed out these kinds of people. He knew that many of His followers were there for the benefits, not necessarily to draw closer to God. The use of parables was His way to make sure that those hearing the gospel had a genuine desire to be saved.

Exposing counterfeiters is the purpose of the parable that we find in the 13th chapter of Matthew.

Another parable He put forth to them, saying: "The kingdom of heaven is like a man who sowed good seed in his field; but while men slept, his enemy came and sowed tares among the wheat and went his way. But when the grain had sprouted and produced a crop, then the tares also appeared. So the servants of the owner came and said to him, 'Sir, did you not sow good seed in your field? How then does it have tares?' He said to them, 'An enemy has done this.' The servants said to him, 'Do you want us then to go and gather them up?' But he said, 'No, lest while you gather up the tares you also uproot the wheat with them. Let both grow together until the harvest, and at the time of harvest I will say to the reapers, "First gather together the tares and bind them in bundles to burn them, but gather the wheat into my barn." (Matt 13:24-30).

What This Parable Tells Us

Tares in a crop look similar to wheat, although somewhat smaller and black. When mixed in with wheat and eaten, it causes dizziness, intoxication, or even paralysis. Because it is deeply rooted with the wheat, it cannot be separated until the harvest for fear of uprooting the wheat as well[7].

Jesus used this parable to inform us that there is an ongoing attack, relentless in nature, trying to destroy us. Satan is infiltrating the church with his imposters when we are not looking, and because they are unidentifiable it makes it nearly impossible to weed them out. Counterfeit Christians with a counterfeit anointing can cut corners to get to a high level of success rapidly. Their blending in to the scenery gives them access to places and people that would not be the case if they were to be exposed abruptly.

These "holy" counterfeiters become a continual thorn in the flesh, clouding our judgment when they constantly question our decision-making abilities. They are difficult to discredit because of their powerful gifting. They are able to produce at a high level and consequently are highly respected. Because of their reputation, we come to the conclusion that they are not only anointed of God but approved of Him as well.

It is in the process of time that their lack of fruit exposes them and pulls their covers. They can no longer hide behind their gifting and anointing because the bottom line is, under all of those pretty leaves there is no fruit. A tree without fruit is useless in the kingdom of God.

Now in the morning, as He returned to the city, He was hungry. And seeing a fig tree by the road, He came to it and found nothing on it but leaves, and said to it, "Let no fruit grow on you ever again." Immediately the fig tree withered away.
(Matt 21:18-19)

My Encounter with Counterfeiters
In high school I had the opportunity to play varsity football for one of the best schools in our area. When I enrolled at El Rancho High in Pico Rivera, California, the football team was only two years removed from a national championship. The entire city lived and died with what

73

happened on the football field every Friday night in the autumn. Just to think that I was going to be a part of this sports juggernaut sent goose bumps down my spine.

For the next three years, I dedicated myself completely to the game that I loved ever so much. There wasn't anything that I was not willing to do to help prepare me to be the best that I could be. The harder I worked, the more successful I became, with the awards coming in bunches. Towards the end of my career, my goal of winning an athletic scholarship to a Division I university was unfolding right before my eyes. To my amazement, I had an offer from my favorite school, the University of Southern California, one of the most prestigious, well decorated programs in the entire United States.

It was at the same time that Christ came knocking on the door of my heart. In the back of my mind, I knew I owed Him one, because at the age of 5 the Lord had miraculously healed me of polio. On the other hand, I believed I was young enough to get my football career out of the way before I dedicated myself unto God. Never did it enter into my mind that I could do both at the same time. I was a one-talent man and I knew my limits. All through my life, although handicapped, my success came from dedicating my life to one thing at a time. That was the secret to my success.

I knew in my heart of hearts that I could not play college football with the same dedication and serve God at the same time. Because of this understanding, a decision had to be made to let go of one or the other. When I did finally make that choice to live for God, leaving my football career by the wayside, much to my chagrin the greatest opposition that I faced came from Christian people. Time and time again, I was told that playing college football would only enhance my soul-winning capabilities. I would be able to influence far more people this way than if I chose not to play. I was constantly reminded that my fame would open the door to the hearts of the unsaved and eventually to God. The effect their conversations had on me was mesmerizing. I found myself somewhat dazed, confused, finding their words very much intoxicating. I realized then that these counterfeiters were having the same effect on me as tares had on wheat.

My Unsettled Heart

As sensible as their arguments sounded, I was still having problems reconciling those assumptions. These counterfeit Christians were toying with my mind. The Scripture in Matthew Chapter 6, verse 24, adamantly states that it is impossible to serve two masters. Any attempt to do so causes a loving of the one and hating of the other.

No one can serve two masters; for either he will hate the one and love the other, or else he will be loyal to the one and despise the other. You cannot serve God and mammon. (Matt 6:24)

I understand that literally, "mammon" means riches. Yet, I believe the definition of riches spreads further than money itself. The problem that must be considered is that fortune usually follows fame, and I didn't need that kind of grief.

Furthermore, attempting to do both would be breaking one of the greatest commandments given to man: *You shall have no other gods before Me* (Ex 20:3). Playing football wasn't a game to me, it had become a god.

There was one last point to consider that bothered me to no end. If I used my playing abilities and fame to win people to Christ, I in actuality would be winning them to me, not Him. That on its own merit is deceitful and comes under the definition of counterfeit. My fundamental purpose in life is to draw less attention to me, with all the attention going to Him. I believe if we will lift up the Lord,

Mammon = riches

He Himself will draw all men unto Him. He really doesn't need our help.

The hunger to succeed has downright compromised our thinking. The pressure brought on by the "mixed multitudes" has put such a strain on our beliefs that we have begun to present a faith that is "seeker friendly."

Counterfeit anointing is the craze of this generation because it is so easy to be had. With a good education and a bag full of talent, who needs a genuine anointing? Our preachers are taking messages off of the Internet, tweaking them, and then preaching them as originals and getting away with it. Our teachers diligently prepare lessons that are "politically correct," making sure that no one is offended by the word of God. Finally, our musicians get into the mix by offering us music with worldly beats and rhythms to excite us because that's what we were used to out in the world. They justify this manner of ministry by using the name of Jesus, and say that they are sincere. Forget the fact that the Babylonians begged the Hebrew musicians to play their music because of its uniqueness and anointing. We all have our reasons as to why we do what we do and they all bring us to ask the same question. Why do we live in an age that lacks powerful anointing? Why are there so many scoffers and mockers continually desiring an easier walk with God? Why are we willing to replace the original anointing with a replica that will not cost us so dearly?

Returning to Our Roots

If we are ever going to see the anointing produce the signs and wonders that the first century Church experienced, our focus must return to its roots. We must lift up the name of Jesus the way our forefathers did. In its simplicity it is powerful enough to bring this entire world to its knees. We don't need Madison Avenue techniques; we're not looking for Hollywood-type antics. Music industry persona shouldn't have a place in our worship services. We need a move of the Holy Ghost by lifting up the name of Jesus. Don't make the same mistake Rehoboam made, replacing the truth of God and His anointing with a counterfeit. It not only cost him his kingdom and his legacy, it ultimately cost him his life.

End Notes

[1]   Ex 9:1-5

[2]   Ex 9:8-12

[3]   Ex 9:13-26

[4]   Ex 10:1-15

[5]   Ex 10:21-23

[6]   Unger's Bible Dictionary, Plagues of Egypt

[7]   Fausset's Bible Dictionary, Tares

CHAPTER 6

Inheriting the Earth With Meekness

Blessed are the meek, For they shall inherit the
earth.   (Matt 5:5)

If there was ever a title of a chapter in a book to be found out of place, it is this one. How in the world does the subject of meekness find its way in a book about anointing? It has as much in common with anointing as pro-life supporters do with pro-choice advocates. Absolutely nothing! The Scripture above draws the same response, because on the surface it appears to be a contradiction. If we look at it from a worldly point of view, there are no leaders in our time who rule with meekness. It is with an iron fist or with a reckless abandon that allows them to rise to the top of their game. Their cutthroat strategies and innovative ideas hurtle them into the stratospheres of success, breaking new barriers as they pass others by. That being said, inheriting the best this world can offer rarely will go to the meek.

When the Lord takes the time to leave us Scriptures that at first glance don't make sense, it behooves us to look a little bit deeper. We cannot take them at face value, because if we do we have the possibility of missing out on a hidden blessing. The words meek or meekness are the words we will focus on and see if we can find the key that will unlock the treasure well-hidden from our understanding.

Understanding Meekness

I think in order to understand meekness in the biblical sense, we must take time to dissect the word from a global perspective. There are words in the English vocabulary that rhyme with meekness and give us a better understanding of how the world perceives this godly trait. Meek not only rhymes with weak, but it also sounds very much like a word used negatively, the word geek.

The geeks of this world are never taken seriously because they don't conform to the norm. They may be superior in areas of intellect, but because of their lack of social skills they stand alone. Geeks are not considered to be a "man's man," therefore the opposite sex has a difficult time getting romantically involved. They may have an IQ of a genius, but their street cred adds up to zero.

The "weak" part of the definition is as equally disturbing. Meekness has always been considered a feminine trait, and no man in his right mind would want that label attached to him. A meek man therefore would be envisioned as a limp-wristed, effeminate-talking, mama's boy who could not fight his way out of a paper bag. Taking into consideration the various cultures that condemn this sort of behavior amongst their male population, meekness found in men is not readily accepted.

It is with this in mind that the Church of today has a difficult time seeing meekness in any other way. It may be one of the fruit of the Spirit that the book of Galatians speaks about. Nevertheless, our use of meekness is usually reserved for our ladies.

If I were to tell you the greatest heroes of the Bible were indeed meek, I sense that you would have a difficult time believing this as well. I'm talking about people like Elijah, Peter, and Isaac. This list could also include

Samson, Joshua, David, and all the rest of the great warriors throughout the Scriptures. Of course the list would not be complete if we were to exclude Abraham, the Apostle Paul, and Jesus Himself. Yet when these great men of God come to our mind, meekness is not the first thing we think of. Anointed maybe, meek never. Attributes like no nonsense, go getting, decisive, or cutting edge are the characteristics we like to use to describe the heroes we would so like to emulate. In reality though, these men I have mentioned, among others, truly were meek, we just don't know it. At the end of the chapter we will come back to this statement and I believe that you will have a completely different outlook.

Defining Meekness

It is time to put a definition to the word meekness as God would see it. The paradox of this definition actually comes from where I discovered it. Meekness was being used in reference to the 1985 Chicago Bears Super Bowl winners. Look at the blog Kevin Seifert wrote for ESPN.com describing those same Bears.

> *"The 1985 Chicago Bears were known, in equal parts, for their dominant defense and outsized personalities. The Bears' blitz-happy "46" defense spurred them to a 12-0 start, a 15-1 regular season record and the largest margin of victory in a Super Bowl at the time. And a roster that included three Hall of Fame players, five All-Pros and nine Pro Bowlers gave us some lasting and unique images."*

With all that testosterone being thrown around, you would think that being labeled meek was an insult, but really it wasn't. You see, that 1985 Bears squad was harnessed and/or controlled by one common goal. At the beginning of the season, they set out to become the best team in pro football. Sacrificing their own wills, egos, and personal goals allowed them to achieve their main objective and to go down in history as one of the greatest football teams ever.

Meekness then, in God's eyes, is having the ability to be harnessed or controlled by the Spirit (Anointing) of God. By the same token, if you harness a wild horse, with much training he can become a thoroughbred. Man has found ways to harness our wild rivers, resulting in an abundance of electricity. Scientists have used the harnessing of atoms as well to invent atomic power. Do you want to know what you get when we, the children of God, are harnessed by His anointing? **THE IMAGE OF CHRIST!**

In trying to find our way in God's kingdom, the choices we make are made without knowing what to really ask for. We are so power-hungry in nature that we are swallowed up by its influence, blinding us to the opportunities to receive something better from God. One must take into consideration that when power is allotted to us, we must also bear in mind that great responsibility comes as well.

There have been various times in my life when I have been confronted by whiners bellyaching that they too could produce great miracles if they had the same power that had been granted to me. To this I have always answered in this fashion. It would do them no good to obtain great power from God if they could not be harnessed by His anointing. I say this because there are so many "out-of-control" Christians today, using their gifts when it is not the will of God. They take something that was provided for good and contaminate it for bad.

Jesus: Always under Control

Even Jesus Himself understood the concept of perfect timing, growing in grace until His entire life was under control of the Spirit. This came from a man who knew no sin and used the wilderness experience, 40 days in the desert, to learn what obedience was all about.

For we do not have a High Priest who cannot sympathize with our weaknesses, but was in all points tempted as we are, yet without sin.

(Heb 4:15)

Place yourself in His shoes for a moment. Even though He was the Son of God, sinless and on a mission to give His life for humanity, Satan did the best he could to stop that from happening. Imagine the temptations that Jesus faced even before the wilderness experience. Surely there were occasions when He could have used His godly powers for good. Providing food for the poor, raising a friend from the dead who was fatally ill, countless of scenarios daily presenting themselves to give a free rein to His glory. But meekness reeled Him in time and time again. It was the determining factor in allowing Him to keep His anointing under wraps and not begin His ministry before its appointed time.

There is one thing in common that I find in most gifted people. They honestly believe that their gifts should be on display publicly 24/7, regardless of the consequences. It is the reason why many pastors are leery to encourage "gifts of the Spirit" ministries to blossom. There has been more harm than good done when these out-of-control enthusiasts do not use the word of wisdom to harness their sudden outbursts. Consequently, things are revealed in public that should have been kept private. Reputations are damaged to the point that many of them are beyond repair, and the prophetic ministry gets a bad rap. Meekness is the fruit of the Spirit designated from heaven designed to not only minimize these errors but to stamp them out altogether. Realizing that there is a greater need for the body of Christ to use this particular gift, it is important to learn how meekness enhances the kingdom of God.

Saving the Lost
The most essential use of meekness we find in His kingdom is when it is used to help save the lost.

In meekness instructing those that oppose themselves; if God peradventure will give them repentance to the acknowledging of the truth;
(2 Tim 2:25 KJV).

When religious arguments come our way, doctrinal or otherwise, there is such an innate desire to win our argument that all we can think about is saving face. We are not interested in the revelation one might gain, but much more having to explain the losing of an argument before our peers. A "win at all costs" philosophy overshadows our good intentions and we find ourselves out-of-control, finally bringing an embarrassment to our lives that is difficult to recover from. We must remember that truth without meekness offends.

To speak evil of no man, to be no brawlers, but gentle, shewing all meekness unto all men.
(Titus 3:2 KJV)

It is interesting to note the word Titus uses in the KJV to describe what not to be when dealing with all men. The word "brawlers" is a great picture word. I say that because when I see that particular word, my mind goes back to my childhood and my love for cartoons. Popeye was my hero, and of course his nemesis Brutus was utterly disliked. My recollection of Brutus was that he was the epitome of a brawler. He was always picking a fight with Popeye, many times for no reason at all, just to fight. One thing I could

84

not understand for the life of me was the constant battling to win the heart of Olive Oyl. She really wasn't all that. Oh my, I've gotten distracted and I must get back on track. It goes without saying that we use the same philosophy in our soul-winning techniques. We foolishly use the Acts 2:38 doctrine as an ax, ripping people to shreds. Then if that is not enough, when they are knocked to the ground, rendered somewhat helpless, we pull out our two 38s to blow them away. While our pride convinces us that we have won a great battle, in reality we have lost the war.

A Great Lesson Learned

I learned a great lesson from a pastor friend of mine who was starting his first pastorate a bit of a distance from where he was living. When settling in, he realized there was a great need to find a Christian school for his children. The city really only had one school in the area that utilized the same curriculum used in the school back home. The only drawback in enrolling his children here was that the school was not of like faith. Convinced that this inconvenience was not as important as his children's education, he enrolled them there anyway.

He took the time to get to know this denominational pastor, inviting him to lunch every so often. As much as he wanted to delve into doctrinal issues, the Holy Ghost had encouraged him to wait. He sensed strongly in the Spirit to form a strong friendship with the pastor before speaking to him about certain issues.

Some time had passed and their meetings together became more frequent. One day out of the blue, the denominational pastor invited him to speak at a weekend camp sponsored by the local church. After receiving a green light from the Lord, he asked the denominational pastor if there was a particular theme he wanted him to follow. The pastor responded with a "whatever the Lord gives you." It was then that he felt confident to preach a series of messages that dealt with the oneness of God.

Long story short, the camp ended with the denominational pastor slain in the Spirit, speaking in other tongues as he received the Holy Ghost. When he had regained his composure, he confidently took his place behind the pulpit and boldly proclaimed that he had just received a revelation of the oneness of Christ. He then announced to his congregation that he would ask the visiting speaker to baptize him in Jesus' name, and asked if there were any other takers. That same day, about 30 other members were baptized in water alongside their pastor.

If meekness had not taken control of my pastor friend's emotions, he probably would have misspoken at a time the denominational pastor was not ready. It would have fallen on deaf ears, probably breaking up their friendship, without another opportunity to do so. Meekness saved the day again.

Helping Our Brethren

The next important reason God has chosen meekness was to provide help when our brethren are in trouble.

> *Brethren, if a man be overtaken in a fault, ye which are spiritual, restore such an one in the spirit of meekness; considering thyself, lest thou also be tempted.* (Gal 6:1 KJV)

Restoration in times past was a difficult concept for the church to grasp. If my memory serves me right, it was not even in the vocabulary of most churches. It is amusing to think that when I was a child, our congregation used to sing a song from Psalm 136 that repeated the word "mercy" in all 26 verses. The song leader would sing the first portion of the verse, followed by the congregation singing in unison the phrase, "for his mercy endureth forever." This song in reality took forever to sing and was one of my least favorites. The saddest thing was that most people who sang it with such vigor did not have a merciful bone in their body. I say this because the general rule in dealing with sin was: one strike and you're out. This rule took on a more adamant stance when pronouncing judgment on the so-called "unforgivable" sins. My father fell under this category when committing adultery, and as a result was excommunicated for life. The church in its ignorance was out-of-control, as much as Saul was when he persecuted the church. In his mind, he was cleansing the world of people who did not believe the right way. It wasn't until the Lord knocked him off his high horse literally that he was set straight.

Our Church in the 60s

I was about 10 years old when what I am about to recount happened in our local church. To this day, it is something that I have never forgotten. In order for you to understand the situation as it unfolded, I need to go back to the 1960s to let you in on how things functioned in those times.

The church was literally in a black-and-white mode. What I mean by that is everything that was worn to church was either black or white. There was not much style or diversity because everyone pretty much wore the same thing. For the men, black pants, black shoes, black socks and a black tie were the requirement. Our shirts were always white. For the women, black skirts and/or dresses, black closed-toe shoes, and a white blouse were the norm.

Males and females were segregated. From the platform looking out to the congregation, the males were seated on the left and the females on the right. It did not matter if you were married, couples did not sit together. There was also a particular order that we had to sit in. The youngest always sat in the front pew, followed by the primaries and juniors.

The youth group occupied the next couple of pews, with the married men sitting in the back. The same order on the other side of the church for the women was practiced.

There was a special place in the back of the church, separated from the rest of the congregation, for those who walked in late. Before you sat down in this section, you were asked by one of the ushers to go up to the altar and pray. It was somewhat embarrassing and considered paying a penance for being late. As you made your way back to your seat, you would be greeted by smug looks and demoralizing snickers. It was the price that had to be paid for your lack of discipline.

The services themselves were drawn out, many times extending to the midnight hour. Powerful moves of God were not uncommon, and we as children had to get used to the fact that we were going to be there for quite some time. There is an old idiom that "children must play," and we were no different. We would have to find something during the service that would occupy our attention. Glad to say our congregation did not disappoint.

There were several things going on simultaneously that kept our eyes glued on the altar. First of all, when the choir sang, there was a particular song a young lady sang that always caused a ruckus. At a particular point in the song, she would always faint. For those first-time visitors who did not know this, they were easy pickings when we bet them this would happen. What was even more amusing and mind-boggling was when the Spirit of God completely took over the service. The running, jumping, dancing, and shaking under the anointing was something to behold. But there was a particular young lady who, when she began her dance, had us completely captivated. I say this because she made her way from one side of the altar where the women were supposed to be, to the other side where the men had their place. Without opening her eyes, she danced to the other side where her boyfriend was sitting and when she got right in front of him, passed out on his lap. To this day, we never figured out how she did it.

Finally, the highlight of the service came when the "holy rollers" started to do their thing. This ministry was reserved for men only, because under the anointing they would fall to the floor and begin rolling from one end of the altar to the other. When this started to happen, those of us in the first row would pick a brother and cheer him on as if we were at the track betting on horses. There were times that we really got into it, and I'm sure as we were jumping up and down, rooting for them, the rest of the crowd probably thought that the Holy Ghost had fallen upon us as well. Now that you understand the climate of the church in those times, I will explain how God uses meekness to help our hurting brethren.

An Unforgettable Event

On a Sunday night right before the preaching was to begin, I hightailed it to the restroom. On my way out, I noticed one of the young ladies sitting in the back. I figured she walked in late and was forced to sit there. Because I really needed to go, I didn't pay too much attention to it. When the altar call was given that evening, she hurriedly made her way to the front, kneeling right before the pulpit. I noticed as she cried out onto God she was completely broken. What I thought strange was that no one came to help her pray. When the Spirit of the Lord died down and almost everyone went back to their seats, she was still there alone, weeping bitterly. At long last, the ladies' president knelt down at her side and began to pray with her. Within a matter of moments, that young lady abruptly got up, running out of the church, never to be seen again.

Several years had passed when, in a conversation with my mom, I asked her what really had happened that night at the altar. She said that in so many words, the ladies' president whispered this in the young lady's ear. *"Get your filthy, good for nothing life out of here. Because of your sin, you are doing nothing more than polluting this altar. If you know what's good for yourself, leave now and don't ever come back."*

I have always believed that the altar of God was a place for repentance. If that is so, and I know that it is, that ladies' president was completely out-of-control. In other words, she was drastically lacking meekness. The Scripture in Galatians admonishes us to restore each other in the spirit of meekness, considering our own lives lest we fall into the same trap. A failure to obey can have deadly consequences. The young lady who never came back found another church willing to restore her life back to Christ. What happened to that proud ladies' president? Woefully, she died an early death.

Jesus' Wise Counsel

The fruit of meekness was so important to the Lord that He mentioned it in a statement He made when He wanted His disciples to learn the most important asset in His life.

Come unto me, all ye that labour and are heavy laden, and I will give you rest. Take my yoke upon you, and learn of me; for I am meek and lowly in heart: and ye shall find rest unto your souls. For my yoke is easy, and my burden is light.
(*Matt* 11:28-30 KJV)

The Lord could have taught them how to cast out demons or even raise someone from the dead. But in retrospect, the greatest lesson the Lord truly could give them was to understand that meekness was the one trait that allowed Him to be as dynamic as He was. The Spirit always had control of His emotions, thoughts and actions.

That being said, I believe we now can go back to the heroes we discussed at the beginning of the chapter. At that time, I made a statement that these heroes of the faith were in reality "meek" men, we just didn't know it. As you have read through this chapter, I believe you can now agree with me that this is true. Being controlled by the Spirit of God was one of the most powerful things that all these men had in common. Meekness was at the forefront of their victories and was the difference-maker in their lives. Having a better understanding of this fruit of the Spirit should help us make a paradigm shift, one that truly believes:

Blessed are the meek, for they shall inherit the earth. (Matt 5:5)

CHAPTER 7

Obtaining A Plain Wrapped Anointing

Blessed are those who hunger and thirst for righteousness, For they shall be filled.

(Matt 5:6)

As the deer pants for the water brooks, So pants my soul for You, O God. My soul thirsts for God, for the living God. When shall I come and appear before God?

(Ps 42:1-2)

For all of you spiritual carpetbaggers, shame on you for skipping the first six chapters. I know that the temptation to get down to brass tacks is overwhelming, yet as you thumb through this chapter, I'm sure that you'll be somewhat disappointed in what it takes to attain a plain wrapped anointing. It boils down to two things that I can actually dovetail together. One is hunger and the other is passion. With a passionate hunger, a plain wrapped anointing can be had. Now, for the rest of you who are still interested in ascending to this level of relationship with God, give me some time to take both words apart and open the door to your understanding.

Hunger is first up on the agenda, and rightfully so. According to the World Hunger Education Service in their 2011 report, in round numbers there are 7 billion people in the world. Thus, with an estimated 925 million hungry people in the world, 13.1 percent, or almost 1 in 7 people are hungry. These statistics do not even take into consideration the malnourished of the world. According to the most recent estimate that Hunger Notes could find, malnutrition affects 32.5 percent of children in developing countries one of three. Geographically, more than 70 percent of malnourished children live in Asia, 26 percent in Africa and 4 percent in Latin America and the Caribbean.

For most of us, these numbers don't mean anything. I say that because the majority of those reading this book have never gone hungry. For all those 24-hour restaurants available to us at a whim, it would do us some good to push away from the table every once in awhile. These statistics may make us feel bad for the moment, but in reality we just can't identify with the rest of the world that goes to bed hungry. Our spiritual condition is equally bankrupt and our hunger to know God has been quenched by our contentment with ministering exclusively in the outer court.

Inner and Outer Court Comparisons

The Old Testament Temple was divided into two parts. The outer court of the Temple was used for daily ministering and sacrifices. The focus of the outer court was ministering to the people. Whatever needs, cares, or problems Israel had were dealt with in the outer court. This is the place in the Temple where the priests were in full view of God's people. It was from this position that all could observe and admire the skill of these men of God as they expertly and proficiently prepared the sacrifices. Winning people over was the primary motivation of these spiritual leaders in Israel. It was grueling and taxing, nevertheless, it was essential in becoming a successful priest.

The inner court, on the other hand, had a completely different focus. The inner sanctuary was divided into two rooms, the Holy Place and the Holiest of Holies. Only the priests were allowed in these sacred areas dedicated to ministering unto the Lord. Of course, ministering unto the Lord was not as glamorous or high profile because everything was done in secret, away from the clamor of the people.

The Levites Go Astray

There was a situation that arose in the time of Ezekiel where the Levites (priests) went astray. The commotion and fuss caused by the outer court had finally taken its toll, and the Levites were ignoring their most important priority.

"And the Levites who went far from Me, when Israel went astray, who strayed away from Me after their idols, they shall bear their iniquity. Yet they shall be ministers in My sanctuary, as gatekeepers of the house and ministers of the house; they shall slay the burnt offering and the sacrifice for the people, and they shall stand before them to minister to them. Because they ministered to them before their idols and caused the house of Israel to fall into iniquity, therefore I have raised My hand in an oath against them," says the Lord GOD, "that they shall bear their iniquity. And they shall not come near Me to minister to Me as priest, nor come near any of My holy things, nor into the Most Holy Place; but they shall bear their shame and their abominations which they have committed. Nevertheless I will make them keep charge of the temple, for all its work, and for all that has to be done in it. "But the priests, the Levites, the sons of Zadok, who kept

charge of My sanctuary when the children of Israel went astray from Me, they shall come near Me to minister to Me; and they shall stand before Me to offer to Me the fat and the blood," says the Lord GOD. "They shall enter My sanctuary, and they shall come near My table to minister to Me, and they shall keep My charge... "And they shall teach My people the difference between the holy and the unholy, and cause them to discern between the unclean and the clean. In controversy they shall stand as judges, and judge it according to My judgments. They shall keep My laws and My statutes in all My appointed meetings, and they shall hallow My Sabbaths.

(Ezek 44:10-16, 23, 24)

Let me summarize this portion of Scripture by saying idol worship caused both the priests and the children of Israel to be judged by the Lord. You would think that with this blatant show of idolatry, the Lord would want nothing to do with them. But this judgment from God is like none other in that the only punishment being rendered is one that restricted the priests from ministering unto God. What a bizarre judgment indeed. It was the Lord's decision to leave these halfhearted lovers of the people to each other.

Of course, the Lord would not be left out in the cold with no one to worship and to minister unto Him. There was a group of Levites, the sons of Zadok, who were given this responsibility. These young Levites were cut in a different mold, perhaps not as popular with the people and surely not as skilled in the outer court sacrifices, but if there was one thing that separated them from the rest of the crowd, it was their ability to worship the name of the Lord.

Modern-Day Levites

The similarities of the Levites and our own ministries are frightening. The parallel becomes more eye-opening when we realize that ministering unto the Lord has been replaced by idol worship. The idols in our case turn out to be none other than our own ministries. We live to minister in the outer court because that is where we enhance our self-esteem. With the platform being our stage, we perform to the crowd in hopes of their approval. What they think and believe is far more important than what God thinks of us, hence our concentration on the outer court. What makes this even more distasteful in the eyes of God is the fact that in order to be successful in the outer court, prayer and consecration are not part of the equation. Sad to say, they are being replaced by experience, education, and talent. What is even more tragic is the fact that we have a great following from our observers in the outer court. Those who choose to follow us follow in our footsteps, and they never really learn how to minister unto God.

I remember hearing a recorded interpretation of tongues that sent chills down my spine. It was said in a way that you could feel the loving kindness of our Heavenly Father, leaving no doubt what side of the fence He stood on when talking about personal relationships.

The interpretation went something like this, *"I came into the room and stood nearby for a long while. I waited for you to recognize my nearness and turn in my direction. I waited for a long while but you were so busy doing what you were doing that you didn't know that I was near. I wanted you to turn because I wanted to tell you that I loved you, but you didn't. You were never aware of my presence."* Notice that this message took place in an everyday setting, not in a church service. The Lord was willing to go out of His way for fellowship with one of His children. Nevertheless, that invitation never had a chance from the get go, because it died in the world of busyness.

97

An Embarrassing Lesson

Years ago, I learned an unforgettable lesson from my son, Timothy. He is not only my oldest child, but he is also my only son. From the time that he was born until now, when he is preparing to marry the love of his life, he has always lived up to his name. The purpose of choosing the name Timothy over George was for that same reason. "Timothy" means "gift from God," and he certainly had the opportunity to demonstrate this on this one particular occasion.

He was 12 years old at the time and just newly converted. I had the great honor of baptizing him at that tender age, remembering that the Lord had already filled him with His Spirit when he was only seven years old. I was trying to mentor him on the ins and outs of the Christian life, helping him to see that prayer was the cornerstone of a great relationship with our God.

With that in mind, we would wake up every morning at the ungodly hour of 3:30 a.m., making our way to the church to pray when the doors opened at 4 a.m. He understood that even though he was not able to keep up with me in the amount of time that I spent in the presence of the Lord, he begged me to let him tag along anyway. After about half an hour of prayer, he would quietly slip out of the church and go back to the car and sleep. We kept this schedule 5 days a week, every week of the year.

At this time in my ministry, I worked a full-time job and then evangelized on the weekends. I did not have the luxury of taking time off, so I would use comp time on Fridays to leave early if I had to fly across the country. As soon as the revival meetings were over on Sunday, I would hurriedly fly back so I could be back to work on Monday morning at 8 a.m. sharp. After doing this for several years, it began to take a toll on me physically, and little by little I was wearing out.

It was on one of these Monday mornings, completely exhausted from one of my trips, that I had made the decision to sleep in. Lo and behold, about the same time I heard a knock at my door. "Dad, are you awake? It's time to get up and go to church." When I did not respond, he continued to knock. "Come on, Dad, we need to go and pray." What in the world can you say to a 12-year-old boy who has that kind of hunger for God? Totally embarrassed and humbled, I got up and we went to church.

Passion vs. Hunger

Blessed are those who hunger and thirst for righteousness, for they shall be filled (Matt 5:6)

As powerful as hunger is to the seeking of God's face, passion is as equally compelling. I do not think that there was anyone in the Bible as passionately in love with God as King David. The words that he chose to describe his love for God sounded more like the words we read in classic love novels.

As the deer pants for the water brooks, So pants my soul for You, O God. My soul thirsts for God, for the living God. When shall I come and appear before God? (Ps 42:1-2)

There is just so much emotion that exuded from this man's heart that it's difficult to believe that anyone could love God that much. It's almost as if he had a "new convert's" frame of mind, one that would wear off in the passage of time. Yet we cannot dismiss the idea that for King David, it was almost a sin not to be in the presence of the Lord.

What can we actually do with his example of unashamed adoration and his obvious transparency? Are we to reject it as an anomaly or accept the fact that our expressions of worship should follow the same pattern?

Spiritual Passion

Let me begin by outlining a meaning for the word passion. Passion is any kind of feeling in which the mind is powerfully affected or moved. It can be a vehement, commanding, or overpowering emotion. It is believed to be that feeling that moves the mind and will to take action[1]. If we put it in spiritual terms, a passion for God refers to our desire, longing, zeal, affection, craving, or hunger for godly things. It then sounds very much like the feelings a person experiences when deeply in love.

The negative experiences that many have had in the past with passionate love have left a bad taste in their mouths, to the point where they begin to rationalize their lack of passion in their lives with God. They then come to the conclusion that feelings are deceptive and cannot be trusted. They go overboard in proclaiming that it's best to trust in the Bible because the Bible is objective, therefore there is no deceit involved. Standing on their soapbox, they admit that the greatest commandment is this one:

> *You shall love the LORD your God with all your heart, with all your soul, and with all your strength.*
> (Deut 6:5)

But, they will not go as far as to include passion with the loving of our God because it goes against their grain and it is the safest way to prevent a broken heart. A case can be made for this type of thinking when they assert that love is actually obedience and not a feeling, which of course they can prove with Scripture.

> *If you love Me, keep My commandments. ...He who has My commandments and keeps them, it is he who*

100

loves Me. And he who loves Me will be loved by My Father, and I will love him and manifest Myself to him." ... *"If anyone loves Me, he will keep My word; and My Father will love him, and We will come to him and make Our home with him.*
(John 14:15, 21, 23)

It could not be stated any plainer than this, and the fact that the Lord Jesus Christ Himself said these words carries a lot of weight. Furthermore, a time-tested truth seems to back up this argument. Correct feelings always follow correct actions, and if that is not the case, obedience to the Word of God always trumps feeling any day.

What Love Is Not
As convincing as this argument is, it does have a fallacy. Obedience without passion is not love. It borders more on the line of discipline or self-will. You can't take passion away from love and still have love. There is one argument I can make that would close the case for the rest of eternity.

If you talk to any disgruntled wife about a woeful marriage, if she is truly honest with you, she will admit that there is one thing at the root of her problems. Actually, if this one obstacle could be overcome, then everything else that is lacking in the marriage could be put up with. You may ask her if there is a lack of provision on the husband's part. Is he a good provider? No she will say, that's not the problem. What about being a good daddy to his children? No, she will say, he is very good with the kids. Is there a lack of respect for you, or does he abuse you in any way? No, he does all the right things at all the right times. Then what is so lacking in your marriage that you find yourself in the doldrums? Almost always, she will admit that there is no longer any passion in their marriage. She remembers the romantic rendezvous during their time of courtship. Her thoughts go back to the days of handwritten love notes and flowers for no particular reason. She will continue to meditate on the days when holding hands was such a big deal. But now they are nothing more than distant memories, ones that have been held captive by the duties of marriage and child-rearing. The chances of those days returning are slim and next to none.

A Godly Complaint

If there were to be a complaint that the Lord Jesus Christ would have with His children, it would be very similar. I cannot say with all honesty that we have become the epitome of the second coming of the children of Israel. Nevertheless, I believe there is something about us that has the Lord yearning for more. It's not that we are not faithful in our church attendance or that we don't make a concerted effort to pay our tithes and offerings. Surely He understands that we are but flesh, and there are periods of time that we don't pray or study His word the way we should. But like that wife who longs for a romantically passionate husband, the Lord only asks of us to serve Him with that same kind of passion. Going through the motions just won't cut it. It's got to be an all out, passionate show of love that will turn the head of our spiritual Father.

I would love to say that the passion I have for God today originated from my relationship with Him, but that was not the case. My passion for things in general actually began at about the age of nine. As a child growing up without a father at home, I was always looking for hero figures, especially ones in church. Worshiping God for me had always been the highlight of going to church, because in those days I did not understand the sermons that were being preached in Spanish. Consequently, I lived for the worship portion of our services. It was then that the desire to learn how to play the trumpet found a lodging place in my heart. Two of my uncles had this wonderful gift, and I cannot tell you how many times I was held spellbound by their ability to play that instrument for the glory of God. With that in the back of my mind, I enrolled in music class. The greatest obstacle I had to overcome was my handicap (I suffered from polio as a five-year-old, and my upper extremities were left withered), because I was not strong enough to push the valves with my right hand. When I came to class the first day, picking up the trumpet with the wrong hand, my instructor did not try to correct me for fear of putting a damper on my enthusiasm. Knowing that the odds were stacked against me, I went into my "overachieving" mode and I practiced and practiced like a man possessed. In actuality, I was possessed, possessed with a passion to succeed. Long story short, by the next year, as a 10-year-old I was the best trumpet player in the entire district. When all of the schools got together for a district concert, we recorded an album where I had the opportunity to play two solos. I was the star of the show, so to speak. It was at that stage in my life that I began to understand what passion could do for someone who did not have all the tools to succeed.

My Passion to Succeed Continued

In an earlier chapter, I briefly mentioned the love that I had for the game of football. I would like to expound on that a little because it was one of the few things in my life that I was extremely passionate about. Early on, I made a decision to fully concentrate and dedicate my life to something that would provide a good education for me, and if things turned out, perhaps a profession as well.

I don't know if it was a lack of understanding or being naïve, but I actually believed that if I worked hard enough without letting anything distract me, I could win a Division I scholarship to any university in the United States. For the next four years, there was nothing I was not willing to do to reach that goal. My extensive training produced many days spent alone and countless solitary moments. With four years of nonstop training, I realized my goal by accepting a full scholarship to play for the University of Southern California.

It was then that I would learn an invaluable lesson about how a passionate heart should be reserved only for the Lord Jesus Christ. (Let me take a sidebar right now and talk to someone who is madly in love with another person. Be careful who you give your heart to, because if it is broken, the recovery from it will not be as easy as you think.) Now, let me get back to the story. When I elected to leave my football career to serve the Lord, never in my wildest imagination did I think that that decision would have such an emotional impact on my life. I had never had anything that I loved so much taken away in my life, and emotionally I was falling apart. I fully understood what God was asking of me, and yet the pull of playing the game had a stranglehold on me. On one day I was sure of my decision, the next day I wasn't. No teenager at the age of 17 should have to make those types of decisions.

Still Vivid in My Mind

What I am about to write happened almost 40 years ago, and I still remember it as if it happened yesterday. I had just turned in all of the equipment that was given to me by USC and was on my way home, holding back tears as I walked through the campus for the last time. When I got to my car, I could not hold back any longer. After a period of time, I gained my composure but the confusion still lingered and I was hurting really bad. I needed an answer from God, one that would be so clear that there would be no doubt as to what direction my life would take me from that point on.

On the interchange between the Harbor Freeway and the Santa Monica Freeway, my answer came in the form of a song titled, "Lovest Thou Me." Because at that time I was not adept in my knowledge of the Scriptures, the Lord used a song to minister unto me. One phrase of the song continued to pass through my mind over and over again. It simply asked the question, "Lovest Thou Me More Than These?" I responded to Him that day with the same lyrics sung in the song, "Oh Precious Lord I Love Thee More Than All of These, More Than Fame, More Than Wealth, More Than the World."[2] Immediately the tears streamed down my cheeks, and I began to speak in tongues as the glory of God fell upon me. Never did I doubt my decision from that day forward.

Satan's Harassment Continued

There is one point that I would like to make about using our passion for other things outside of our love for God and the repercussions. Although I was sure about the direction God wanted me to go in, that did not mean that Satan would stop his badgering to make me rethink my decision. I was constantly reminded by the enemy that my passion for God did not come anywhere near the passion I had displayed in my football career. It was hard to argue the fact when living for God was a completely different life than I was accustomed to. The perks that came from a privileged life that was always in the public's eye were sorely missed, and being humbled by God constantly brought back a longing for those glorious days.

For the next couple of years, I stood painfully in front of the mirror every morning, asking God when would the time come that I loved Him with the same passion I had had for football? This struggle was my continual partner that became more aggravating when I continued to receive scholarship offers from other schools. All I could do was put myself in the hands of God and pray that within time and with His grace, I could cross over to the other side.

As I am writing this now, it's somewhat emotional because I can still picture the day when looking in the mirror, I knew I was different. Without a certain event or a special word from God, I just knew that my passion for Him had tipped the scales and I had arrived at the place that I so longed for when I initially gave my heart to Him.

The Best-Kept Secret

This is where the benefit of a passionate hunger comes into play. When most people inquire how I got started in a signs and wonders ministry, they are somewhat shocked when I tell them I never asked for the gifts that flow so freely in my life. The secret to a powerful plain wrapped anointing is not found begging for His gifts, but rather in utilizing the time in His presence to seek His face. To this day, in all I have experienced in Him, nothing compares to spending time at the foot of the Master. I try as often as I can to utter this to my Lord as I enter into His presence in prayer. I say, "Lord, You know that the time we spend together will be more important than anything else I can do for You this day." Plain and simple perhaps, but it's always verbalized with a passionate hunger. The words that David wrote in Psalm 42 are so much clearer to me now as I have lived these years for Christ. I really do understand the feeling of, "when shall I come and appear before God?" With hunger and passion I seek His face. Is that how you approach the throne of God?

Blessed are those who hunger and thirst for righteousness, for they shall be filled. (Matt 5:6)

End Notes

[1.] Webster's Dictionary, passion
[2.] Bill Gaither

CHAPTER 8

Distracted From Your Destiny

I press toward the mark for the prize of the high calling of God in Christ Jesus. (Phil 3:14 KJV)

Distractions, Distractions, Distractions!!! Wouldn't the world be a better place without them? If your attention has been drawn or been directed to different objects or in different directions at the same time, then you, my friend, have been distracted.

Have you ever driven on the freeway, looking for a particular off ramp in an area that was unfamiliar to you? You are running late and don't have time to miss the off ramp. You are sure by the directions that have been given to you that you are very close to your destination. All of a sudden, out of nowhere a rock bounces from a truck in front of you and comes flying at your windshield. The suddenness of the impact distracts you from your concentration. It is but for a brief moment, but is long enough to allow you to pass that off ramp. When you finally calmed down, believing that no harm had been done, you kept on going but never found that off ramp, frustrating you to no end.

Distractions Are a Part of Life

Being distracted in different directions at the same time happens more than we would like to think. Why is it when a deadline has to be met that all hell breaks loose? Here you are, trying to finish this project on time, but it seems that the whole world is against you. The phone begins to ring nonstop. The computer decides to crash and all that you had worked on has been lost. At that same moment, your teenage daughter waltzes in, pleading for more money because what you have given her isn't enough to buy that outfit for graduation. If that isn't enough, your mother-in-law, who you don't get along with because of her incessant complaining, decides to visit, bringing her schizophrenic son along for the ride. Your untrained dog gets into the act, jumping onto the desk and pooping all over it. He then leaves his signature with a puddle of pee soaking your work. On top of all of this, the eczema that you thought you had under control begins to act up and the itching becomes unbearable. That is exactly how Satan works in our lives.

Whether we realize it or not, distracting us away from God is Satan's main objective when dealing with us. It does not have to be of seismic proportions, but if he can bump us just enough to knock us off line, it could be enough to never realize our destiny. We will be shoved from the perfect will of God, to the permissive will of God, to eventually out of the will of God. There are so many Christians today who have never received the best that God has to offer, simply because for a brief moment they were distracted.

Where to Focus Our Energies

When the Apostle Paul admonished us to press towards the mark, it was imperative to do so in our seeking of God. We are to become insistent, thrusting our way towards the throne room without yielding to distractions, pushing forward with a non-relenting single-mindedness.

*No, dear brothers and sisters, I am still not all I should be, but I am **focusing all my energies** on this one thing: Forgetting the past and looking forward to what lies ahead,*   (Phil 3:13 NLT)

Our focus is to be all-encompassing, one that would expend every ounce of our fiber to concentrate solely on our destiny. It entails having a good "forgetter." A good "forgetter" not only forgets the bad, but also the good as well. Sometimes it takes more energy to forget the good so that we do not rest on our laurels. In seeking the will of God in our lives, it would be wise to take this approach:

Give me neither poverty nor riches — Feed me with the food allotted to me; lest I be full and deny You, and say, "Who is the LORD?" Or lest I be poor and steal, and profane the name of my God.
                    (Prov 30:8-9)

In order to focus all our energies on the Lord, we must entertain an anointing that is plain wrapped. We are talking about an anointing that will defer all the attention from us, to the one who deserves all of that attention, the Lord Jesus Christ.

What do we have to possibly gain from such an effort? Heaven, of course! With our priorities set in order, we can then receive our reward. It is the highest calling of God a Christian could ever receive, our final resting place. No more dying there, no more sickness and pain, and best of all, Jesus will be there. No more distractions, just Jesus!

but lay up for yourselves treasures in heaven, where neither moth nor rust destroys and where thieves do not break in and steal for where your treasure is, there your heart will be also.

                    (Matt 6:20-21)

The Foolish Virgins

Distractions are what got the foolish virgins (Matt. 25:1-13) in trouble, because they never took their assignment seriously. They had been given one and only one responsibility, and that was to keep their lamps well oiled.

Those who were foolish took their lamps and took no oil with them, (Matt 25:3)

Somewhere down the line they became distracted and delayed keeping their lamps at full strength. The Scriptures never tell us what it was exactly, but their attention was directed elsewhere and they neglected their most important duty.

The oil (a type of anointing) was taken for granted and provisions for replenishing it were not taken. Having enough oil for show was sufficient. They were not ready to go out of their way, lugging around extra weight that was not a necessity. There really wasn't a need to go to extremes.

It is amazing how, when we do not prepare, that which we have not prepared for comes to pass. Because we do so much traveling, I always ask my wife to pack extra clothing. Whether it is for unexpected weather or the fact that at times pastors will extend our stay by continuing the revival, we always try to be prepared. You don't know how many times that has saved us.

On the other hand, our dependence on our efficiency can distract us as well. My schedule is constantly changing, for the reason that we are forever on the go. Knowing this, I will always make sure to schedule my prayer time into my day. When that time is going to be taken away by a schedule change unbeknownst to me, the Lord will attempt to wake me up a couple of hours earlier to get that time in. I say "attempt," because there are times I do not get up, knowing that I have another time set aside for that purpose. Like the foolish virgins, I reason with God that there is no cause to go to extremes.

A Foolish Mistake

It is at this point in our Christian lives that our walk with God parallels that of the foolish virgins. Taking a page out of the Laodicen church, they walked with lukewarmness, unabashedly flaunting their worldliness without shame. "No one is going to tell me what to do, I do what I want" was the motto of the day.

And at midnight a cry was heard: 'Behold, the bridegroom is coming; go out to meet him!' Then all those virgins arose and trimmed their lamps. And the foolish said to the wise, 'Give us some of your oil, for our lamps are going out.' But the wise answered, saying, 'No, lest there should not be enough for us and you; but go rather to those who sell, and buy for yourselves.' And while they went to buy, the bridegroom came, and those who were ready went in with him to the wedding; and the door was shut. "Afterward the other virgins came also, saying, 'Lord, Lord, open to us!' But he answered and said, 'Assuredly, I say to you, I do not know you.' (Matt 25:6-12)

When the bridegroom finally came, they were not prepared. As they ran off to buy more oil, their meeting with the bridegroom was delayed and consequently they were rejected. They were just distracted for a moment, which then delayed the biggest encounter of their lives, which in turn left them with nothing.

Superficial Distractions

The superficial things used in our lives to distract us seem to do the most damage. The Old Testament story of Achan surely testifies to this fact. As the army of Israel destroyed the city of Jericho, Achan, one of its warriors, was distracted by the glitter and glamour of the spoils. His heart began to covet these riches so much that he had to have them for his own. He made a decision to steal and then hide them so that no one would know.

It is astounding to think how many people believe they can hide from God. Adam, in the Garden of Eden, was the first one to make this foolish attempt. He tried to cover his sin literally by using fig leaves to conceal his naked body. When that did not work, he was forced to 'fess up, leaving God no choice but to judge him. Adam would find out firsthand just how harsh the judgment of God could be. He not only lost out on living in a perfect world, more importantly he lost that special relationship he had with God.

Now, let's get back to Achan. The distraction didn't allow him to think straight, so he buried it, believing that in time the problem would just go away. What he didn't realize was that his theft had brought a curse upon all of Israel. It was his selfish act that caused the 36 deaths of his compatriots.

> *Joshua said to Achan, "My son, I beg you, give glory to the LORD God of Israel, and make confession to Him, and tell me now what you have done; do not hide it from me."* (Josh 7:19)

Achan found out that worshiping God with a clear conscience was an impossibility. Sin will always separate you from the Lord with an inability to worship.

Give unto the LORD the glory due to His name;
Worship the LORD in the beauty of holiness.

(Ps 29:2)

Achan knew that there was nothing holy about his thievery, thus not being able to give God the glory. Confessing his wrong was the only manly thing to do. He was then judged and taken out of the city with his family to be stoned to death, paying a greater price than the riches he had stolen. His destiny was not only short-circuited, so was that of his family as well.

Esau's Hunger Does Him in

Achan's affinity for riches may not have been so superficial in your eyes, but what about giving up a birthright for food? Esau found himself distracted because of his hunger. The fact that he was in the field all day hunting and was dead tired greatly factored into his poor decision. Being attacked at our weakest points is a surefire way for Satan to take advantage of us. But what was he thinking? He was giving up a whole lot more than what he was receiving in return. His birthright was worth a double portion blessing, he would have become the head of the family, but more importantly it was the blessing that put him in close relationship with Jehovah[1]. Yet he still despised it, it was worthless in his eyes.

And Esau said to Jacob, "Please feed me with that
same red stew, for I am weary." Therefore his name
was called Edom. But Jacob said, "Sell me your
birthright as of this day." And Esau said, "Look, I
am about to die; so what is this birthright to me?"
....And Jacob gave Esau bread and stew of lentils;
then he ate and drank, arose, and went his way.
Thus Esau despised his birthright.

(Gen 25:30-32, 34)

113

When Tiredness Distracts Us

When tiredness distracts us, we belittle our salvation because our hunger leads us in other directions. Even if those other directions are not considered blatant sin, they are far enough away from the will of God to knock us off track. Our time spent in His presence is then put on hold, delaying His glory in our lives. Our destiny then is redirected and we find ourselves settling for plan B.

Timing with God is everything. For that same reason Satan works overtime, triggering delays of all sorts. Whether they are uncontrollable circumstances, extending a waiting period, or just Satan being Satan, they are all part of his bag of tricks. Moments of indecision can knock the timing of God's will out of whack. Uncontrolled circumstances play a great part in delays as well. Satan, the master of delays, is many times directly responsible for the mayhem.

Our sensitivity to God through His anointing becomes our security blanket. How so? Being in tune with God always puts a damper on distractions and delays. A prayed up child of God is Satan's worst nightmare.

The effective, fervent prayer of a righteous man avails much.   (James 5:16)

The Unnamed Prophet

If only the man of God we find in 1 Kings 13:1-32 had understood this lesson. For no particular reason, the Scriptures do not mention his name. All we know about him is that he was a prophet mightily used of God. He arrived in Bethel, denouncing unlawful sacrifices just as King Jeroboam was about to offer one. He prophesied the death of the king and the destruction of the altar. When the king attempted to have him seized, his hand became paralyzed at the same time the altar was split in half, so the king pleaded for mercy. After the prophet healed

Jeroboam's hand, the king invited him back to the palace to reward him. The prophet refused for this reason:

> *But the man of God said to the king," If you were to give me half your house, I would not go in with you; nor would I eat bread nor drink water in this place. For so it was commanded me by the word of the LORD, saying, 'You shall not eat bread, nor drink water, nor return by the same way you came.'" So he went another way and did not return by the way he came to Bethel.* (1 Kings 13:8-10)

Unlike Achan, this man was not easily distracted. He was on a mission, he understood his purpose, and in obedience he carried it out. But a strange thing happened on his way home. He was met unexpectedly by another prophet who made a similar invitation to abide in his home. He was then somehow distracted by this elderly prophet, perhaps his reputation preceded him, we really don't know, the Scripture never really says.

> *He said to him, "I too am a prophet as you are, and an angel spoke to me by the word of the LORD, saying, 'Bring him back with you to your house, that he may eat bread and drink water.'" (He was lying to him.)* (1 Kings 13:18)

A Regrettable Decision

Without consulting God he took the prophet's word and spent the night in Bethel. At the dinner table, the Lord spoke to the older prophet, who then pronounced judgment on the disobedient man of God.

> *Now it happened, as they sat at the table, that the word of the LORD came to the prophet who had brought him back; and he cried out to the man of*

God who came from Judah, saying, "Thus says the LORD: 'Because you have disobeyed the word of the LORD, and have not kept the commandment which the LORD your God commanded you, but you came back, ate bread, and drank water in the place of which the LORD said to you, "Eat no bread and drink no water," your corpse shall not come to the tomb of your fathers." (1 Kings 13:20-22)

On the way home, the man of God was met by a lion and was killed, never fulfilling his destiny.

It does not seem fair that a man could be judged when he has been lied to. Deceit and dishonesty are not par for the course, yet they are allowed to bring down this innocent man of God.

For such are false apostles, deceitful workers, transforming themselves into apostles of Christ. And no wonder! For Satan himself transforms himself into an angel of light. Therefore it is no great thing if his ministers also transform themselves into ministers of righteousness, whose end will be according to their works.

(2 Cor 11:13-15)

We should not be so surprised by this level of deceit. It is the same tactic that Satan has employed since the beginning of time. It is our responsibility to make sure that what we are receiving from heaven truly comes from God.

Beloved, believe not every spirit, but try the spirits whether they are of God: because many false prophets are gone out into the world. (1 John 4:1)

The testimony of this prophet ends with a strange twist. We never got to know his name.

116

A Baffling Experience

Early in my years of evangelizing, the Lord brought someone my way who would have a great impact on my life. I had been preaching a revival for a couple of days in a particular church when I stumbled upon something that I had never experienced. As I was working the altar one night, making my way from one side to the other, the closer I got to a particular man, the more I began to gag over a stench that was emanating from him. Never had I ever smelled anything so nauseating. It got to the point that if I got any closer, I was afraid that I would vomit right then and there.

As I began to retreat, the Lord spoke to me and assured me it wasn't what I thought it was. Of course, I could not make heads or tails of the situation, so the Lord needed to be very blunt about His explanation. He said, "If what you smell is so bad, then why aren't the people around him gagging as well?" I stopped to think about what He just said and realized there was more to this situation than I had originally thought. In reality, I was the only one who could smell what I smelled. It wasn't a physical problem causing my confusion; it was one originating from the spiritual realm. It was a divine marking placed on this man's life that was to separate him from the rest of God's children. In a manner of speaking, it was God's way of showing me that even if I was to pray for him, nothing was going to happen because God had already judged him. It was only after the service that I understood why.

Shortly after the service ended, I received a note to meet this man in private. We found an empty Sunday school room where we did talk. He began the conversation, admiring my ministry and encouraging me to grow in God's grace. It was then he unfolded a story that I will never forget.

God Sends Me a Warning

He said, "I too at one time was an evangelist with a signs and wonders ministry. It was incredible what God had done through His anointing and I never ceased to be amazed. It happened so quickly that my head could not stop spinning. As a rising star in the sky, my ministry grew from nothing to the most wanted preacher in our organization. My calendar was filled months and months in advance. The offerings I received were enough to live on very comfortably. The more I dedicated myself to Him, the more He responded with spectacular miracles. I started to overextend myself because I liked the attention and the money. Little by little, it all began to catch up with me and I started to let go of my prayer life. The reason why I was willing to do that was because the gifts of the Spirit God had given me had come to a place of perfection. (When that happens in the child of God's life, he can produce miracles without an ounce of prayer.) What I didn't realize was this. Although I was working as powerfully as I had in the past, without prayer I could not discern seducing spirits."

Now the Spirit speaketh expressly, that in the latter times some shall depart from the faith, giving heed to seducing spirits, and doctrines of devils

(1 Tim 4:1 KJV)

"It was at this point in time that I let down my guard and was seduced into an affair, actually a one night stand. From one night of indiscretion, I contracted AIDS and now I am dying."

It was then that I realized why the Lord had not healed him when I had prayed. Sad to say, the judgment of God had fallen upon him, and similar to the prophet who was fooled, he too fell into that category. This does not mean that he was not forgiven of his sin. Nevertheless, his body was to be destroyed so his soul could be saved.

In the name of our Lord Jesus Christ, when you are gathered together, along with my spirit, with the power of our Lord Jesus Christ, deliver such a one to Satan for the destruction of the flesh, that his spirit may be saved in the day of the Lord Jesus.

(1 Cor 5:4-5)

I found out a short time later he had died. It was a death far sooner than what God had planned for his life. His destiny was sidetracked by distractions, distractions that eventually destroyed him.

Where is your focus? Are you completely dedicated and devoted to the Lord Jesus Christ? Are you enthusiastically consecrated to the point that everyone you know would agree? Does your commitment to Christ border on the fringe of fanatical? If not, we need to look again at the apostle's words about where our energies should lie.

*No, dear brothers and sisters, I am still not all I should be, but I am **focusing all my energies** on this one thing: Forgetting the past and looking forward to what lies ahead, **I strain to reach the end of the race** and receive the prize for which God, through Christ Jesus, is calling us up to heaven.*

(Phil 3:13-14 NLT)

Reaching the End of the Race

This is where our energies should be centered, reaching the end of the race. It should be done with an effort that causes us to strain (i.e., to go beyond a usual, accepted, or proper limit or rule). Pressing, pressing, and pressing some more till we reach that mark of the high calling of God. Don't let the distractions of this world, be what they may, knock you off the right track. Your destiny is worth a whole lot more than that.

End Notes

1. International Standard Bible Encyclopedia, Birthright

CHAPTER 9

Not on My Watch

So I sent messengers to them, saying, "I am doing a great work, so that I cannot come down. Why should the work cease while I leave it and go down to you?" (Neh 6:3)

On the scale of 1 to 10, how boring would the job of a watchman be? Think about it for a moment! Here he is, a man pacing up and down the high tower on the city wall or on a desolate hillside. Back and forth he goes, walking over the same steps time and time again. His greatest challenge in life is to wage the war against boredom, yet his job was one of the most important ones in the camp of Israel. His main responsibility was to prevent any surprise attacks from the enemy. Knowing that he was the first line of defense, he bravely guarded the lives of the entire city. He would have to be a passionate man to take this type of job, because only a man with passion could take this job seriously.

He basically worked pretty much by himself, and certainly his time could not be wasted on daydreaming. In his solitude, this man had to focus entirely on the land outside of the walls without being distracted by the monotony of his post. He had a great vantage point to see where others could not see, and his view on the tower allowed him to see oncoming trouble from great distances. Finally, negligence by the watchman could only mean one thing: loss of life. If he didn't do his job and do it well, the enemies of Israel would easily overtake the city.

Responsibilities of a Spiritual Watchman

We as the body of Christ must have this same watchman's mentality. The responsibility to keep the church in the will of God should fall upon all of us, regardless of position or stature. Only a true anointing will help us accomplish this assignment. This picture below should be enough motivation to comply with God's orders.

"So you, son of man: I have made you a watchman for the house of Israel; therefore you shall hear a word from My mouth and warn them for Me. When I say to the wicked, 'O wicked man, you shall surely die!' and you do not speak to warn the wicked from his way, that wicked man shall die in his iniquity; but his blood I will require at your hand. Nevertheless if you warn the wicked to turn from his way, and he does not turn from his way, he shall die in his iniquity; but you have delivered your soul.

(Ezek 33:7-9)

Our spiritual eyes must be the first line of defense, discerning with our spirit the attacks of the enemy. We can never lose our passion to defend the truth. It is this same truth that our forefathers fought and died for, making sure it would not perish under pressure but be passed on in its purity to the next generation. They understood that the truth would set them free, and consequently were willing to give their lives for it.

"If you abide in My word, you are My disciples indeed. And you shall know the truth, and the truth shall make you free." (John 8:31-32)

Our minds must be made up to defend our position, come what may. There is a generation coming behind us that will need a powerful anointing to accomplish His will, thus protecting this anointed truth should be our number one priority. It is vitally important to take the position that we are doing a great work. Our efforts must not be reduced by outside pressure. We cannot come down and lower ourselves to please others. More so, we must continue to fight, continue to pray, and continue to unleash an unadulterated anointing that will not only break the yoke, but shatter the enemy's assault on the truth. We are the spiritual watchmen God has called to do this work and we will not fail, NOT ON OUR WATCH!

Nehemiah's Concern for Jerusalem

Nehemiah had to make a stand when he realized that the city of Jerusalem was in disarray. In his anguish upon hearing how his country was destroyed by fire, he humbled himself completely before the Lord and began a four-month-long time of consecration. It was at this time that seeking God's face through prayer and fasting was the only way he knew to remedy the situation. Note that this period of sanctification was extended until the Lord was ready to launch him out, completely anointed for the job.

So it was, when I heard these words that I sat down and wept, and mourned for many days; I was fasting and praying before the God of heaven. And I said: "I pray, LORD God of heaven, O great and awesome God, You who keep Your covenant and mercy with those who love You and observe Your commandments, please let Your ear be attentive and

Your eyes open, that You may hear the prayer of Your servant which I pray before You now, day and night, for the children of Israel Your servants, and confess the sins of the children of Israel which we have sinned against You.   (Neh. 1: 4-6)

As you can see from the Scriptures above, Nehemiah wept bitterly for his nation and for his God's intervention. His prayers before the throne of Jehovah were relentless and his intercession continued both day and night. His watchman spirit allowed him to persevere when the rest of his countrymen had all but given up. His prayer was at long last answered and King Artaxerxes granted him permission to go back to Jerusalem to rebuild its walls. The first task of importance would be to convince the remnant of the need to rebuild the walls.

Then I said to them, "You see the distress that we are in, how Jerusalem lies waste, and its gates are burned with fire. Come and let us build the wall of Jerusalem, that we may no longer be a reproach." And I told them of the hand of my God which had been good upon me, and also of the king's words that he had spoken to me. So they said, "Let us rise up and build." Then they set their hands to this good work.   (Neh 2:17-18)

Time for a Fight
It was at this point in time the heavy opposition began. Any time you set your mind to do a great work for God, you will encounter a resounding resistance, countered by an ongoing antagonism that will produce an undaunted hostility united to destroy your efforts. That's exactly what Nehemiah encountered when news broke out that the walls of Jerusalem were going to be rebuilt.

There is a saying that goes, "disaster comes in threes," and in Nehemiah's case the same held true in the form of the three stooges, Sanballet, Tobiah, and Geshem. They took a page out of the art of conflict, inflicting the first phase of controversy by using mocking, ridicule, and intimidation. The problem with this form of discord was that Nehemiah was totally convinced that the hand of God was upon him. He was able to shake off the opposition without batting an eyelash, and because God had given him watch over this project, nothing less than victory would be accepted on his watch.

The game of "chicken" intensified, because that is Satan's modus operandi; he never goes down without a fight. They saw that morale was low, so there was a devilish plot to attack Jerusalem and cause confusion amongst the builders. The plan was to divide and conquer.

Then Judah said, "The strength of the laborers is failing, and there is so much rubbish that we are not able to build the wall." And our adversaries said, "They will neither know nor see anything, till we come into their midst and kill them and cause the work to cease." So it was, when the Jews who dwelt near them came, that they told us ten times, "From whatever place you turn, they will be upon us."
(Neh 4:10-12)

Nehemiah retaliated with prayer. He set a watch against them without ceasing. Watching and praying, praying and watching, they are truly an unbeatable combination. I believe that the Apostle Paul could identify with Nehemiah's burden. Nehemiah's predicament placed him in one similar to Paul's when imprisoned; he passionately pleaded for all of the saints.

...praying always with all prayer and supplication in the Spirit, being watchful to this end with all perseverance and supplication for all the saints — and for me, that utterance may be given to me, that I may open my mouth boldly to make known the mystery of the gospel, for which I am an ambassador in chains; that in it I may speak boldly, as I ought to speak. (Eph 6:18-20)

When You're in Over Your Head

Nehemiah found himself in a dilemma beyond his capabilities. He was a cupbearer by trade, not a stonemason, so the finer points of building were beyond his comprehension. It was because of these shortcomings that he sought the Lord for revelation. This is what this anointed man of God received in prayer.

So it was, from that time on, that half of my servants worked at construction, while the other half held the spears, the shields, the bows, and wore armor; and the leaders were behind all the house of Judah. Those who built on the wall, and those who carried burdens, loaded themselves so that with one hand they worked at construction, and with the other held a weapon. Every one of the builders had his sword girded at his side as he built. And the one who sounded the trumpet was beside me. Then I said to the nobles, the rulers, and the rest of the people, "The work is great and extensive, and we are separated far from one another on the wall. Wherever you hear the sound of the trumpet, rally to us there. Our God will fight for us." (Neh 4:16-20)

This one simple strategy orchestrated with a little "kneeology" confused the opposition and they peacefully retreated in defeat. There was one thing that the enemies of Jerusalem could all agree upon, and that was that one anointed man of God, Nehemiah, was the key to Jerusalem's success.

I can certainly identify with Nehemiah in that I have been confronted with situations where I could truly say, "I was in over my head." A walk of faith is one in which control of the situation is always deferred to the Lord, which makes for some pretty hair-raising experiences (although I am bald).

A Request That Incensed Me

I could not believe what I was hearing when the Lord asked me to target my energies in Spanish ministries. I not only could not speak the language, but as a third-generation Hispanic I had an attitude against my Spanish-speaking brethren. This extreme abhorrence could be easily compared to the hatred found amongst Jews and Arabs. They are half-brothers, yet they cannot stand each other. My disdain for them (Spanish speakers) came from the mocking I received from English-speaking people. They would clump American-born Mexicans with non-English-speaking Hispanics, and that used to drive me crazy. I grew up more "gringo" than some Anglos. I may have had brown skin on the outside, but I definitely fit the definition of "Coconut" (brown on the outside and white on the inside) and was proud of it.

That being said, when my new assignment of ministering to the Hispanic community was made clear, I was in complete shock. The thought kept on swirling around in my head, "How could God be so cruel?" The only way that I could deal with this so-called injustice was to humble myself and pray. It did not make matters any easier when, in attempting to speak the Spanish language, I butchered it completely. The jeers, teasing, and laughter were unmerciful, yet in spite of that I had to trudge on.

It was this humbling experience that brought me to my knees with a season of prayer and fasting like I had never ever known. In constant need of the Master's help, I clung to Him for dear life. I found out much later that this breaking period in my life was used to fortify my character.

God was able to break me of my bad attitudes and at the same time give me a love for my people; one that I never thought was possible.

Nehemiah's Watchmen Mentality

Nehemiah's mettle and resolve were more than his enemies could take, thus a plot to assassinate him was put into play. They came to the conclusion that if he would just come down and reason with them, it would give them the best opportunity to kill him. The fallacy in this line of reasoning was, you can't reason with a fool.

> *Do not answer a fool according to his folly, lest you also be like him.* (Prov 26:4)

Nehemiah's final response to his detractors was repeated four times because they would not take no for an answer. His watchman mentality kicked in with these words:

> *So I sent messengers to them, saying, "I am doing a great work, so that I cannot come down. Why should the work cease while I leave it and go down to you?" But they sent me this message four times, and I answered them in the same manner.*
> (Neh 6:3-4)

With this frame of mind he, along with the rest of the Jews, was able to rebuild the walls of Jerusalem in only 52 days.

When we review the story of Nehemiah and his success in rebuilding the walls, it is easy to discount his accomplishments because of the advantages that were given to him when he set out on his assignment. From Scripture we know that he was given the position of Governor in that region so that those under his jurisdiction would understand the absolute authority given to him by the King. If ever a man was placed in a win-win situation, it was Nehemiah. Those advantages he enjoyed help us to draw upon our objections of not having what it takes to get the job done. Truth be told, with a watchman's spirit and attitude, anything is possible.

A Remarkable Display of Motherhood

The name Rizpah does not ring a bell when we consider the great women of God in the Bible. Her story is hidden and somewhat lost amongst the portions of the Bible that are dedicated to documenting all of the great accomplishments of King David. Her resume reveals that she was one of King Saul's concubines, or in other words, one of his inferior wives.

As King David inquired of the Lord the reason of a three-year famine in the land, this is God's answer to David's question:

Now there was a famine in the days of David for three years, year after year; and David inquired of the LORD. And the LORD answered, "It is because of Saul and his bloodthirsty house, because he killed the Gibeonites. ...And the Gibeonites said to him, "We will have no silver or gold from Saul or from his house, nor shall you kill any man in Israel for us." ... Then they answered the king, "As for the man who consumed us and plotted against us, that we should be destroyed from remaining in any of the territories of Israel, let seven men of his

*descendants be delivered to us, and we will hang
them before the LORD in Gibeah of Saul, whom the
LORD chose."."*   (2 Sam 21:1, 4-6)

How did Rizpah get involved in this discussion between
King David and the Gibeonites? Two of her sons were
involved in this exchange, to be executed by crucifixion.
Could there not be an easier way to appease the
Gibeonites? Crucifixion was considered in those days as
the most excruciating, agonizing death a man could suffer.
Realizing that the breaking of an oath, King Saul's error, set
off this judgment, the judgment surely did not fit the crime.
Nevertheless, according to the law of Moses, blood
guiltiness resting upon the land could only be expiated by
the blood of the criminal.

*So you shall not pollute the land where you are; for
blood defiles the land, and no atonement can be
made for the land, for the blood that is shed on it,
except by the blood of him who shed it.*
          (Num 35:33)

Rizpah's Vigil Begins
Recognizing that she was a victim of vengeance, she
made a decision to live up to her name (i.e., hot stone[1]) and
with white-hot passion she protected her murdered sons and
the others as well, seven in all. Her unceasing vigilance
included scaling the various crosses by day to ward off
flesh-eating vultures, while at night fighting off the various
wild animals with nothing more than pure grit. It was her
passion that in reality offset her anger. The thoughts of
injustice rolling around in her mind fueled this awesome
display of motherhood. By law, the dead bodies should
have been taken down at sundown (Deu 21:22-23), but it
was vengeance that left them there to rot in the elements.
The bodies were left hanging from the beginning of barley

130

harvest, the sacred Passover season, until the fall of the early rain in October, a period of about six months.

On her watch, nothing and no one was going to even come close to touching those bodies. Watching those bodies blacken, decay and wither, constantly fighting the stench of the rotting, she never relaxed her vigil. She was going to obtain justice if it was the last thing that she did.

> *And David was told what Rizpah the daughter of Aiah, the concubine of Saul, had done... So he brought up the bones of Saul and the bones of Jonathan his son from there; and they gathered the bones of those who had been hanged. They buried the bones of Saul and Jonathan his son in the country of Benjamin in Zelah, in the tomb of Kish his father. So they performed all that the king commanded. And after that God heeded the prayer for the land.* (2 Sam 21:11, 13-14)

Notice that the curse upon Israel was not lifted even when David complied with the Gibeonites' request. The fact that David broke another law (i.e., leaving the dead bodies hanging after sundown) infuriated the Lord so much that He still wouldn't honor David's act of restitution. It wasn't until this dedicated mama went all out to protect her sons that David paid attention, owning up to his mistake and rectifying it. It was one little lady with a watchman's spirit, who would not take no for an answer, who finally brought justice for her sons.

The Greatest of Watchmen

The greatest watchman we must consider, of course, is none other than the Lord Jesus Christ. His one and only mission in life was watching over our salvation plan. If there was anyone ever focused on accomplishing His purpose in life, it was our Savior. His plan to find His way to the cross was masterful. On one hand He brought attention to Himself by creating unmatched miracles, yet on the other hand He allowed such a ruckus amid His unorthodox ministry that His legacy was always enveloped in controversy. His presence alone was enough to convince a paltry few that He was the Messiah the Jewish nation was waiting for. While He was fulfilling scripture by healing the sick and raising the dead, He did it in such an unassuming way, with a plain wrapped anointing, that it still left doubts in the minds of the majority of His detractors.

His ministry came to a screeching halt when He was unjustly accused, judged, and then convicted. Never once did He defend himself opening His mouth, which was in itself a fulfilling of prophecy.

He was oppressed and He was afflicted, yet He opened not His mouth; He was led as a lamb to the slaughter, and as a sheep before its shearers is silent so He opened not His mouth. (Isa 53:7)

He was decisively certain that He would complete His mission no matter how much it hurt. In His mind, He would not be distracted, no not on His watch.

What makes His dedication even more mind-boggling is that He really didn't want to die. His knowledge of the Scriptures made the anticipation of His death even more unbearable. He knew from the outset that His face was to be so disfigured that it would be unrecognizable.

Many were amazed when they saw him beaten and bloodied, so disfigured one would scarcely know he was a person. (Isa 52:14 NLT)

The loss of blood from the scourging and the crown of thorns alone would have killed any man, He knew this as well. He also knew ahead of time that He would pretty much die alone without the support of His disciples, which brought utter dismay to Him. *Strike the Shepherd, and the sheep will be scattered;* (Zech 13:7).

The words uttered in the Garden of Gethsemane sounded very convincing until He went back to the disciples, not looking for help, but rather for a way out.

And He was withdrawn from them about a stone's throw, and He knelt down and prayed, saying, "Father, if it is Your will, take this cup away from Me; nevertheless not My will, but Yours, be done."
(Luke 22:41-42)

When He found them asleep, He went back to pray and the Scriptures say this prayer was more earnest (Luke 22:44) because He didn't even believe His own words. His sweat was as drops of blood, proving that His humanity almost overtook His divinity, but He did the right thing, going to Calvary and dying the most brutal death a man could die.

One Last Failed Attempt
Before the culmination of His death, the chief priests dared Him to come down from the cross.

Likewise the chief priests also, mocking with the scribes and elders, said, "He saved others; Himself He cannot save. If He is the King of Israel, let Him now come down from the cross, and we will believe Him.   (Matt 27:41-42)

If there was ever a lie that was uttered in the history of man, it was this one. There is no way that the chief priests were going to make good on their promise. There was one and only one way the Lord would be able to draw all men unto Him.

And I, if I am lifted up from the earth, will draw all peoples to Myself."   (John 12:32)

True to His watchmen nature, His view from Golgotha's Hill gave Him a vantage point like none other. He saw lost souls that could only be saved by enduring a death that was reserved for the most criminal. His purpose in life overrode His excruciating pain. In other words, humanity would not be lost without a Savior, not on His watch.

Is that the type of passion you have in your walk with God? Where are the watchmen of our generation?

For if the trumpet makes an uncertain sound, who will prepare for battle?   (1 Cor 14:8)

Our battle cry has been lost in ambiguity. Sadly enough, our forces have begun to splinter because the watchman's warnings are not being heard. Is this the generation that will be caught unawares? Hopefully, not on this watch.

End Notes
[1]   International Standard Bible Encyclopedia, Rizpah

CHAPTER 10

Declaring Your Victory

And I will give you the keys of the kingdom of heaven, and whatever you bind on earth will be bound in heaven, and whatever you loose on earth will be loosed in heaven.   (Matt 16:19)

When children of God go into battle against the adversary, it is amazing how our purpose is so easily misconstrued. There are so many warriors who battle for their lives believing God is depending on them to secure a victory. The truth of the matter is that God is looking for "spiritual enforcers," ones who will stand up against the devil to proclaim victory that God has already won. Victory was complete at Calvary when the works of the devil were completely destroyed.

For this purpose the Son of God was manifested, that He might destroy the works of the devil.
(1 John 3:8)

The destruction of the devil was done on a legal level. That means all of the dominion Satan stole in the Garden of Eden, when Adam sinned, was bought back by the death of Jesus Christ on Golgotha's hill. This included physical healing, the lifting of oppression, liberating those under demonic control, and setting the captives free.

This new freedom we have gained is effective if and only if it is enforced. In other words, if we do not stand up to the devil when he tries to intimidate us with his power, then he has all the right in the world to take what we let him take. He will test our knowledge and power just to see what he can get away with.

What is most encouraging to us is the fact that Satan has to honor authority. Our feeble attempt to battle with him on even terms is never taken into consideration. We have every right to look him straight in the eye to declare our victory. There are no ifs, ands, or buts. Declare it by faith and God will back you up.

You will also declare a thing, and it will be established for you; So light will shine on your ways. (Job 22:28)

Declarations Must Be Verbal

If a declaration is going to be effective, it has to be verbal. That may appear to be a redundant statement. Nevertheless, it must be proclaimed verbally because there are many children of God who believe a declaration of the heart and or mind is the needed prerequisite to open the windows of heavenly blessing that they seek.

Let me elaborate on this philosophy for a moment regarding the subject of salvation. Believing in the heart for the salvation of one's soul is only the first step, and those who stop here, stop short.

For by grace you have been saved through faith, and that not of yourselves; it is the gift of God, not of works, lest anyone should boast. (Eph 2:8-9)

136

There is an inference here that salvation comes from the heart and nothing that we do can procure it. That is basically true and not true at the same time. Believing in God for our salvation is very much the same as having faith in God. Believing and having faith are not abstract concepts formulated in the mind or in the heart where they cannot be seen. On the contrary, believing and faith are action words. If people believe and have faith, they should be able to see that with their own eyes. Paul states this plainly in the book of James:

Thus also faith by itself, if it does not have works, is dead. But someone will say, "You have faith, and I have works." Show me your faith without your works, and I will show you my faith by my works... You see then that a man is justified by works, and not by faith only. (James 2:17-18, 24)

Putting our faith to work includes a verbal declaration. Once people repent of their sin and believe with their hearts, they go on to the next step to make it known unto the entire world.

For with the heart one believes unto righteousness, and with the mouth confession is made unto salvation. (Rom 10:10)

This is what is called "putting our money where our mouth is." It is at this time we complete the puzzle of the salvation plan and are baptized in water, seeking His Spirit.

This is in compliance with the words Jesus spoke to Nicodemus in the book of John.

Jesus answered, "Most assuredly, I say to you, unless one is born of water and the Spirit, he cannot enter the kingdom of God. (John 3:5)

Verbalizing Our Faith Is Ongoing

The verbalizing of our faith should not be reserved for only at the time of our salvation. Declaring our victory is an ongoing affirmation, validating the greatness of the Lord in our lives. With sacrifices of praise making their way up to the throne of glory, we joyously honor Him daily.

Therefore by Him let us continually offer the sacrifice of praise to God, that is, the fruit of our lips, giving thanks to His name.   (Heb 13:15)

The author's admonition to us is that we should continually and not continuously offer this sacrifice with our lips. He purposely does not use continuously, because then our praise would get old real quick. What he had in mind when he wrote this scripture was this. Our praise is to be done over and over and over again, that's why it becomes a sacrifice and a costly one at that. Paying a high price for a sacrifice never stopped King David from offering the Lord his best.

... nor will I offer burnt offerings to the LORD my God with that which costs me nothing.

(2 Sam 24:24)

What does the Old Testament burnt offerings have to do with our sacrifices of praise? Everything of course! The writer of Hebrews had to have a working knowledge of Old Testament sacrifices because of his use of the word "continually" in Hebrews 13:15. The burnt offering sacrificed by the priests was considered a "continual" burnt offering (Ex 29: 42). But what allows this Old Testament sacrifice to connect to our praise is that the burnt offering typified the entire consecration of the worshipper to Jehovah[1]. That is the reason why David would not discount his sacrifices unto the Lord. He wanted to make sure that he

138

was sacrificing the best and only the best money could buy, because that is the type of appreciation he wanted to demonstrate before the Lord. Do you think that we should offer Him any less? I really don't think so. Our declarations to Him should not only be verbal but demonstrative as well.

Earlier in the chapter I mentioned how believing and having faith go hand in hand. We already know that without faith it is impossible to please God (Heb 11:6). We must then realize that a faithless declaration does not mean much.

A Hollow Shout

*And when the ark of the covenant of the LORD came into the camp, all Israel **shouted so loudly** that the **earth shook**. Now when the Philistines heard the noise of the shout, they said, "What does the sound of this great shout in the camp of the Hebrews mean?" Then they understood that the ark of the LORD had come into the camp. So the Philistines were afraid, for they said, "God has come into the camp!" And they said, "Woe to us! For such a thing has never happened before. Woe to us! Who will deliver us from the hand of these mighty gods? These are the gods who struck the Egyptians with all the plagues in the wilderness. Be strong and conduct yourselves like men, you Philistines, that you do not become servants of the Hebrews, as they have been to you. Conduct yourselves like men, and fight!" So the Philistines fought, and Israel was defeated, and every man fled to his tent. There was a very great slaughter, and there fell of Israel thirty thousand foot soldiers. Also the ark of God was captured; and the two sons of Eli, Hophni and Phinehas, died.* (1 Sam 4:5-11)

As loud as the shout of Israel was that day, causing the Earth to shake, the truth of the matter was the shout rang hollow. After the initial fear of something they had never ever heard before subsided, they knew for a fact that Israel was backslidden and could not defeat the far superior Philistine army. They manned up and slaughtered 30,000 soldiers without skipping a beat.

This sacrifice of praise was a joke in comparison to that of King David. It cost them nothing to roar at the top of their lungs, hence their performance convinced no one. What made matters worse was that the Ark of the Covenant was taken, as if the Lord were condoning this act of thievery. If the children of Israel were not going to be able to honor God with the first fruits of their praise, then the presence of the Lord might be more appreciated elsewhere.

Faith-filled words, once shot out into the atmosphere, have power like none other. Satan would prefer us to bite our tongue and leave our faith stuck in our hearts. He goes to such extremes in his lies to make us believe that if we are to receive answers from God, we must expend an exorbitant amount of faith.

I believe that the Lord goes out of His way even more so to bless His children. I say that because He has lowered the requirement of receiving miracles from heaven to the lowest degree. It is not a radical, fanatical, obsessive amount of faith that moves mountains in our lives, but a faith not any bigger than the size of a mustard seed (Matt 17:20). That means that anyone willing to launch out with a little bit of faith God has deposited in their life can unmistakably have what they say.

Joshua's Impossible Predicament

Joshua found himself in a predicament that only a miracle could remedy. On top of the fact that he was struggling with his own identity, he had to make heads or tails of his given assignment, which made no sense at all.

There was no one to go to for counsel, because if it were to be made known to the rest of his leadership how the Lord planned to conquer the city of Jericho, I'm sure he would have found little if no support at all. He was going to have to do this one on his own and pray that what he thought was the will of God surely was.

The walls of Jericho were impenetrable. On the outside looking in, these walls were fortified to the max, which made a successful invasion nearly impossible. Considering that Israel was a makeshift army, undermanned and ill-equipped, it could not possibly match the state-of-the-art weapons the soldiers of Jericho boasted in their arsenal. This confrontation was a match made in heaven. The Lord has always thrived on impossible situations, and there could not have been a more impossible one than this.

A declaration of victory was going to be the instrument God used to triumph over Israel's enemies and it would come with nothing more than a shout. For six days in a row, Joshua asked his men to march around the walls of Jericho in silence. I can imagine the heckling and mocking of these hapless soldiers who were doing nothing more than kicking up the dirt. Then came the seventh day and all of Jericho would understand the power of a shout.

But it came to pass on the seventh day that they rose early, about the dawning of the day, and marched around the city seven times in the same manner. On that day only they marched around the city seven times. And the seventh time it happened, when the priests blew the trumpets, that Joshua said to the people: "Shout, for the LORD has given you the city!...So the people shouted when the priests blew the trumpets. And it happened when the people heard the sound of the trumpet, and the people shouted with a great shout, that the wall fell down flat. Then the people went up into the city, every man straight before him, and they took the city. And they utterly destroyed all that was in the city, both man and woman, young and old, ox and sheep and donkey, with the edge of the sword.

(Josh 6:15-16, 20-21)

A declaration of victory cannot be discounted, especially when the Lord has your back. He understands what it is to declare victory when to all intents and purposes the situation appears to be terminating in defeat.

The Lord's Example to Us
The last item on the agenda before He was to gruesomely die was a shout of victory declared from the top of his lungs. It wasn't a shout of agony, dismay, or defeat, as some might have imagined. What it really was, was a voice of triumph. With all of the strength that He could muster, He shouted:

And when Jesus had cried out with a loud voice, He said, "Father, 'into Your hands I commit My spirit.'" Having said this, He breathed His last.

(Luke 23:46)

The power of a shout of victory was not lost in His death. He was just setting the stage for His return, because when He does come back for His church it will be one hallelujah shout of victory.

For the Lord Himself will descend from heaven with a shout, with the voice of an archangel, and with the trumpet of God. And the dead in Christ will rise first. Then we who are alive and remain shall be caught up together with them in the clouds to meet the Lord in the air. And thus we shall always be with the Lord. (1 Thess 4:16-17)

There is one obstacle that continues to rear its ugly head and stops an anointed child of God from receiving the best that heaven has to offer. For some reason or another, breaking tradition is one of our greatest stumbling blocks. These inherited, established, customary patterns of thought put such a damper on our thinking that many times we believe this is the only way of serving God. We must return to the Bible as our infallible source and not depend on what grandpa did back in the day. If the new thoughts, actions, or behavior we are experiencing at the moment can be substantiated from similar biblical examples, what's wrong with pushing tradition aside?

A Startling Moment

Several years ago, I made an altar call where a pregnant woman got in line to be healed. She was suffering from the normal back pains women suffer from when they are expecting. Right before I laid my hands on her, the Lord revealed to me what she was going to have. I excitedly stopped in my tracks and asked her if she knew already what the baby was going to be, because if not, I could tell her what God had revealed to me. I was somewhat startled by her response in that she emphatically said no and did not want to know. For whatever reasons, the Lord did not want me to leave it at that, so I approached her in a different way. I said, "I know you don't want to know what the baby will be, but can I at least tell you how your baby will come out?" She looked at me cockeyed, as if she thought what I was asking was a trick question, but after thinking about it briefly, she gave me the okay. In my nervousness, I told her that the baby was going to come out singing. If there was ever a preposterous statement, it was that one. We all know that physically, this was an impossibility. Because I was taken aback by her initial response, I was so nervous this is what I really wanted to say. Your baby is going to come out to be a singer. What a great difference, huh? She snickered a bit, but then was captivated by the thought that the baby in her womb was going to sing for the glory of God and accepted it that way.

She Had a Change of Heart

After the service was over, she hurriedly made her way to the platform where I was standing. She had changed her mind and wanted to know what the Lord had showed me. I told her that she was going to have a little girl, which drew an unexpected shriek from her. You see, the Lord had blessed her with boys and all she needed was a little girl to make her family complete. She did something that most of us are not willing to do when we receive a prophetic word from the Lord. She opened up her mouth and began to declare her victory. It did not matter if the doctors could confirm this prophecy, she was going to take a step of faith and announce it to the world. And on top of that, her baby was going to sing for the glory of God.

A couple of months passed, when driving down the road, she suffered an accident in her van. The van began to tumble over and over again. When the paramedics arrived, she was bloodied with some broken bones. They hurried her onto the ambulance, knowing that if they did not get to the hospital in time there was a great possibility she was going to lose the baby. In all the commotion, the enemy came onto the scene with his taunting, sarcastic remarks. "Where is your God right now? You know you're not going to get to the hospital in time, so you might as well forget about the little girl God promised you." About the same time, the manifest presence of the Lord entered into the ambulance and a powerful anointing fell upon her. With all of the strength she could gather together, she said something like this, "Satan, the Lord rebuke you! First of all, I am going to get to the hospital in time, then I am going to have my little girl and there's nothing you can do about it." You know what she was actually doing? She was opening her mouth and declaring her victory. Just a little bit of faith being released by this woman was enough to deliver the miracle that she needed so desperately.

When she arrived at the hospital, a doctor came in immediately to check in on her. He hurriedly wrote down some notes and left. It was at this time her pastor walked in the room, and as she was still feeling that powerful anointing she asked him to pray. After a brief prayer, another doctor walked into the room for further examination. As the pregnant lady eyed him, she observed that he was somewhat perplexed. When she asked him if there was anything wrong, he responded that the notes left by the first doctor did not correspond with the examination that he had just given. According to the notes, the pregnant woman should have had some broken bones. But after the more recent examination, the doctor found nothing wrong with her. To this she responded, "Can you take me into the birthing room so I can have my little girl?"

An Unexpected Turn of Events

They rolled her into the birthing room and when the baby was finally born, the strangest thing happened. The little "girl" began to make noises as if she was singing. That caught the attention of everyone in the room, including the doctors and nurses who had never seen anything like this. The Lord then swooped in with His Spirit and with a powerful anointing touched the mother. She said, "Why are you so surprised? Haven't you ever seen a baby give honor and glory unto her God?" I know what I've written sounds too incredible to believe, but then again, that's the kind of God that I serve.

But Jesus looked at them and said, "With men it is impossible, but not with God; for with God all things are possible." (Mark 10:27)

Actually, the best part of the testimony came about three months later when I returned to her local church to preach. After the service was over, she approached the platform to show me her baby. It appeared that she was upset, and because the baby wasn't dressed in girly colors I assumed she was coming to give me a piece of her mind. When she finally got close enough for me to look at the baby, I peered down one last time to see if I could figure out if there was a girl or not. She then asked me if I had remembered her. I had said no, when in fact I really did but I didn't want to face the music. She said there was no way I could not remember because I had prophesied that God was going to give her a little girl. "Really," I said. "What is it?" A little astonished, she responded, "A little girl, of course!" I remember thinking but not really verbalizing it, "Thank God!" Wiping my sweaty brow with my towel, I blurted out a Whew!!!!!!!!!!! I tried to change the subject by asking a common question, "What did you name her?" She immediately responded with a nickname that did not make any sense to me at all. At that time, I did not know the circumstances of how the baby was born, so when she cried out the name, "TUMBLES," it really threw me for a loop. After she took the time to fill in the blanks, I began to give praise to the incredible God I serve. Now, every time someone asked her about the nickname, she had the greatest opportunity to declare victory again and again. Tumbles, who would've thunk it?

Still Not Convinced?

This testimony may have convinced most of those reading this book at the moment, but I'm sure that there are those who still aren't convinced. I say this because laying a solid foundation on experiences without biblical backup is spiritual suicide. But for those of you who go to the other extreme, never venturing out from the Scriptures for a fresh word from God, let me convince you by using His word.

Then Joshua said, "Open the mouth of the cave, and bring out those five kings to me from the cave." And they did so, and brought out those five kings to him from the cave: the king of Jerusalem, the king of Hebron, the king of Jarmuth, the king of Lachish, and the king of Eglon. So it was, when they brought out those kings to Joshua, that Joshua called for all the men of Israel, and said to the captains of the men of war who went with him, "Come near, put your feet on the necks of these kings." And they drew near and put their feet on their necks. Then Joshua said to them, "Do not be afraid, nor be dismayed; be strong and of good courage, for thus the LORD will do to all your enemies against whom you fight." And afterward Joshua struck them and killed them, and hanged them on five trees; and they were hanging on the trees until evening.

(Josh 10:22-26)

A Changing of Tradition

In this portion of Scripture there is a changing of an old tradition. What was customary after the Israeli army had secured a victory was to bring the defeated king inside the city gates and present him before the leader of Israel. As the entire city gathered around to see what came next, the leader, in this case Joshua, would put his right foot on the neck of the defeated king, who by this time was bowed down before Israel's leader.[2]

In this particular occasion, Joshua decided to defer his responsibility to the captains of his army. Whether it was because there were five kings who were brought before him that day or not, the Scripture never is clear on that point. All we know is this, Joshua transferred his authority to these five men. With that authority now in place, they completed the tradition and the kings were then taken out of the city to be killed.

What does an Old Testament tradition and the changing thereof have to do with us in today's kingdom? We all know from studying the Scriptures that Joshua is a type and figure of the Lord Jesus Christ. That means there was a parallel in both of these men of God. There were things Joshua would physically do that the Lord Himself would duplicate in the spiritual realm.

Taking from the tradition that Joshua was accustomed to, we find that Jesus did the same in the Spirit:

And the God of peace will crush Satan under your feet shortly. (Rom 16:20)

Oh, it gets better, my friend. As Joshua was able to transfer his authority to the men in his army, so the Lord has transferred His authority to us as His soldiers.

Behold, I give you the authority to trample on serpents and scorpions, and over all the power of the enemy, and nothing shall by any means hurt you. (Luke 10:19)

There are those who are reading the Scripture above at this time who are not doing the backward somersaults that they should be doing. Why? Because they don't believe this scripture applies to their lives. It is the Scripture in their minds that is reserved for the upper echelon in Christ's kingdom.

Let me put your mind at ease by referring to the Scripture that was given at the beginning of the chapter in Matthew.

And I will give you the keys of the kingdom of heaven, and whatever you bind on earth will be bound in heaven, and whatever you loose on earth will be loosed in heaven." (Matt 16:19)

What These Keys Can Do for You

The keys that have been given to you and me were given to declare our victory. I love the word the Lord chose to use to help us understand there are no boundaries or limits to what He is willing to do in our behalf. "WHATEVER" is a word used so much today in our society that there's no way we could misunderstand its meaning. Whether good or bad, everything in our lives is covered by "whatever." We just need to make up our minds that when God gives us a promise, we can boldly declare our victory before it even happens, because we know God is true to His word. It's time to DECLARE YOUR VICTORY!!!!!!!!!!!!!!!!!

End Notes

[1] Zondervan Pictorial Bible Dictionary, Sacrifice, Pg 739

[2] Manners and Customs of the Bible, Enemies Trodden On, Pg 119

BOOKS AVAILABLE IN ENGLISH

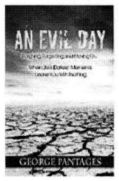

LIBROS DISPONIBLES EN ESPAÑOL

George Pantages Ministries

George Pantages
Cell 512 785-6324
geopanjr@yahoo.com
Georgepantages.com